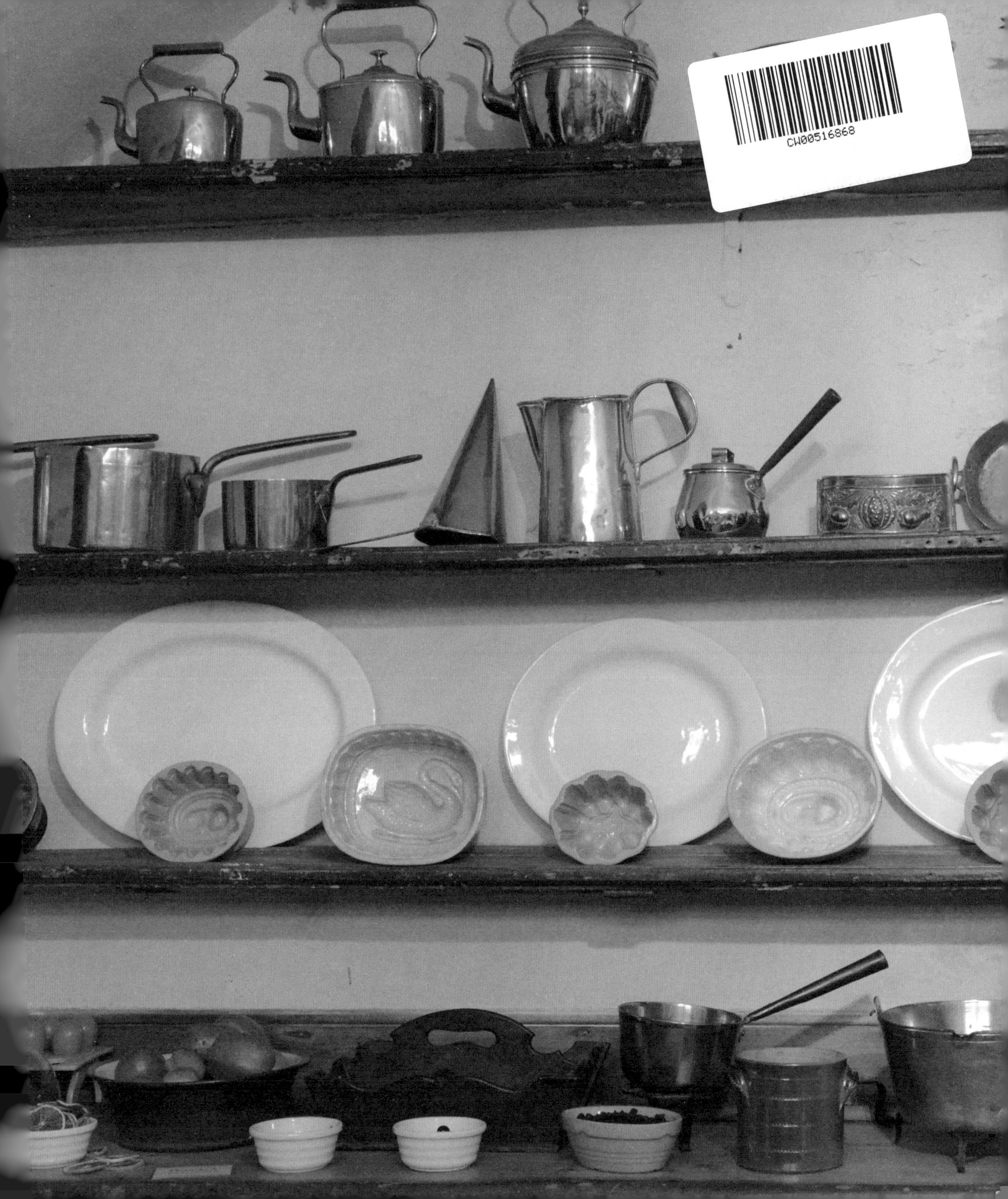

First published in the United Kingdom in 2019 by Balmy Kitchen Publishing.

ISBN 978-0-9574848-2-5

Recipes by Laraine Hare

Photography by Laraine Hare, Jennifer Carlin and Bath Preservation Trust
Book design by Jennifer Carlin

I am very grateful to Janey Abbott at No 1 Royal Crescent Bath (Bath Preservation Trust) for allowing me to use their beautiful images. It is a wonderfully preserved Georgian house and still has its original kitchen with the dresser, kitchen range and Stothert bread oven. There is also a scullery, housekeeper's room and servants' hall. If you are visiting Bath it is an unmissable experience.

Thanks to Alex and David at Old Bank Antiques, London Road, Bath, for their invaluable advice.

Thanks to all at the New Oriel Hall in Larkhall, Bath for their help and support and to all of my friends for helping me to test out these recipes.

Thank you to Dail for proof reading the book with her wonderful eye for detail.

Thanks to Leonie and Tom for being there for me.

Images
Cover: Copper pans from 1 Royal Crescent, photography Jennifer Carlin
Previous page: Dresser from 1 Royal Crescent, photography Jennifer Carlin

A Georgian Cookery Book

Authentic 18th century recipes that
you can prepare in your own home.

CONTAINING

ALL KINDS OF RECIPES AND HOW TO MAKE THEM

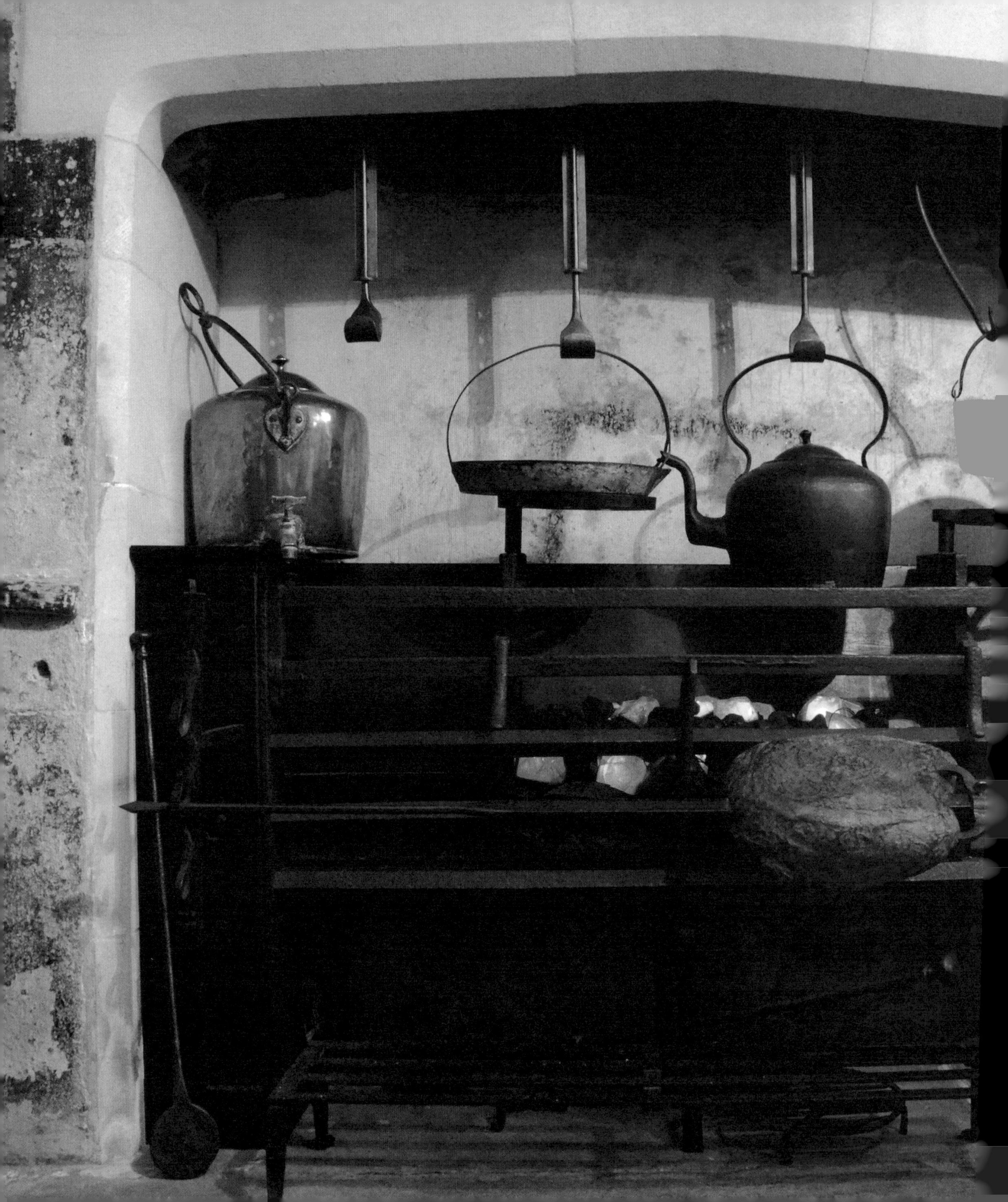

Introduction.

'Custom has lately introduced a new mode of seating. A gentleman and a lady sitting alternately round the table, and this, for the better convenience of a lady's being attended to, and served by the gentleman next her. But notwithstanding this promiscuous seating, the ladies, whether above or below, are to be served in order, according to their rank or age, and after them the gentlemen, in the same manner'.

John Trusler. 1788. 'Rules of the Table'.

In many ways the Georgians were like us; they loved exploring international tastes and dishes, whilst at the same time appreciating locally produced foods. John Nott, cook to the Duke of Bolton, described England as a: *' happy island flowing with Milk and Honey'*, (1723. 'The Cook and Confectioner's Dictionary'.)

Many of the Georgian nouveau riche wanted to provide feasts to impress their friends, in imitation of wealthy aristocrats, but unfortunately most of their cooks were unfamiliar with the fashionable dishes of the time. Cookery books were written to help improve their culinary skills, but those who could afford to employed professionals like William Verral, who ran The White Hart in Lewes. Verral was often asked to teach cooks to prepare dinners for special occasions in the homes of local 'gentlemen'. He complained that they often had inadequate or unhygienic utensils, so he had to take his own along. He was horrified when, asking for a sieve, he was presented with one that had been used for sanding the stairs. When he objected, the cook washed it around in a stockpot containing pork and cabbage and returned it to him as ready for use. (1759. 'A Complete System of Cookery: The Cook's Paradise')

Left: Range from 1 Royal Crescent

The very wealthy sought cooks from abroad, especially France; many chefs came to England with their aristocratic employers, to escape from the horrors of the revolution.

The Prince Regent brought the famous French chef and writer, Antonin Carême, to cook at the Royal Pavilion in Brighton, where the kitchens were so splendid that the Prince personally showed them off to his guests. However, the chef did not stay long as he was unpopular with the kitchen staff, refusing to share the food left over from feasts, traditionally seen as cooks' perks.

A formal dinner was a very grand affair, served around 3.00 in the afternoon, and continuing until late in the evening. There would be two or three courses, each of which could include over twenty dishes, both savoury and sweet, followed by dessert. Sometimes there was a long gap between courses, and Jane Austen described this as producing an 'awkwardness', so that Emma and Frank Churchill were *'obliged to be as formal and as orderly as the others; but when the table was again safely covered, when every corner dish was placed exactly right, occupation and ease were generally restored.'* (1815. 'Emma')

Louis Simond, an American travelling in England, was disgusted by many English eating habits: *'bowls of coloured glass full of water are placed before each person. All (women as well as men) stoop over it,*

sucking up some of the water, and returning it, often more than once, and, with a spitting and washing sort of noise.' He was equally appalled by the use of chamber pots in the dining room: *'The operation is performed very deliberately and undisguisedly, as a matter of course, and occasions no interruption of the conversation.'* (1815. 'An American in Regency England. 1810-11')

Others were concerned with the food itself, which was often adulterated in order to improve its appearance, or to make it go further. Cheese sometimes contained red dye to improve the colour, and used tea-leaves were re-coloured with verdigris (which is poisonous) to imitate China tea. John Farley, the principal cook at the London Tavern, wrote a detailed appendix in his book, describing the most common 'culinary poisons': *'though we do not swallow death in a single dose, yet it is certain that a quantity of poison, however small, which is repeated with every meal, must produce more fatal effects than is generally believed.'* (1811. 'The London Art of Cookery'.)

Despite these problems, many were able to enjoy a wonderful variety of food. Even those on a relatively limited budget could find ingredients that could produce *'an Elegance in Eating no ways inconsistent with Frugality and good Conduct.'* (1733. Sarah Harrison. 'The Housekeeper's Pocket-Book') John Farley has a whole chapter on 'frugal dishes', which includes recipes using cheap cuts such as offal, but also more elaborate recipes such as jugged hare, using an 'old hare'. (1811. 'The London Art of Cookery')

Tobias Smollett wrote of how some managed to *'eat for twelve shillings a week',* consuming foods such as *'sheep's trotters and cow-heel.'* (1771. 'Humphrey Clinker')

For workers living in rural areas, meals were relatively simple. Most would eat their main meal in the middle of the day, using a large cooking pot to cook all of the ingredients together. Many of the poorer rural families caught rabbits to supplement their diet, despite the strict anti-poaching laws of the time.

Benevolent landowners and local parishes would provide feasts for their workers at special times of the year. Parson Woodforde describes his 'frolic' when people came to pay their tithes. *'I gave them a good dinner, surloin of beef rosted, a Leg of Mutton boiled and plumb puddings in plenty.'* This was served with a generous amount of alcohol: *'They had to drink Wine, Punch, and Ale as much as they pleased; they drank of wine 6 Bottles, of Rum 1 gallon and half, and I know not what ale ... We had many droll songs from some of them.* (1985. 'A Country Parson: James Woodforde's Diary, 1759-1802.')

Some were so poor that they ended up in the workhouse, built and maintained by rates paid by wealthy households. The diet fed to those unfortunate enough to live in these grim houses was recorded in detail. For example, in St John at Hackney in the 1750s, there was a daily allowance of:

7 Ounces of Meat when dressed, without Bones, to every grown Person,
2 Ounces of Butter,
4 Ounces of Cheese,
1 Pound of Bread,
3 Pints of Beer
(1951. 'Travellers in 18th Century England.' Bayne-Powell, R.)

Note: Most recipes usually feed between 4 and 6 people, depending on their appetite.

ABOUT THE AUTHOR

Laraine's background is in teaching, including work with children with special educational needs and later with international students at Bath Spa University. She ran a cookery school for five years and created recipes using food produced in the area (published in her first book, Bath's Luscious Larder). Living in Georgian Bath inspired her to research the food that would have been cooked in kitchens of 18th century homes. This led to research trips all over the country to compare kitchens, larders, sculleries, dairies and kitchen gardens, and resulted in this Georgian Cookery Book.

Laraine has an MA in Visual Culture.

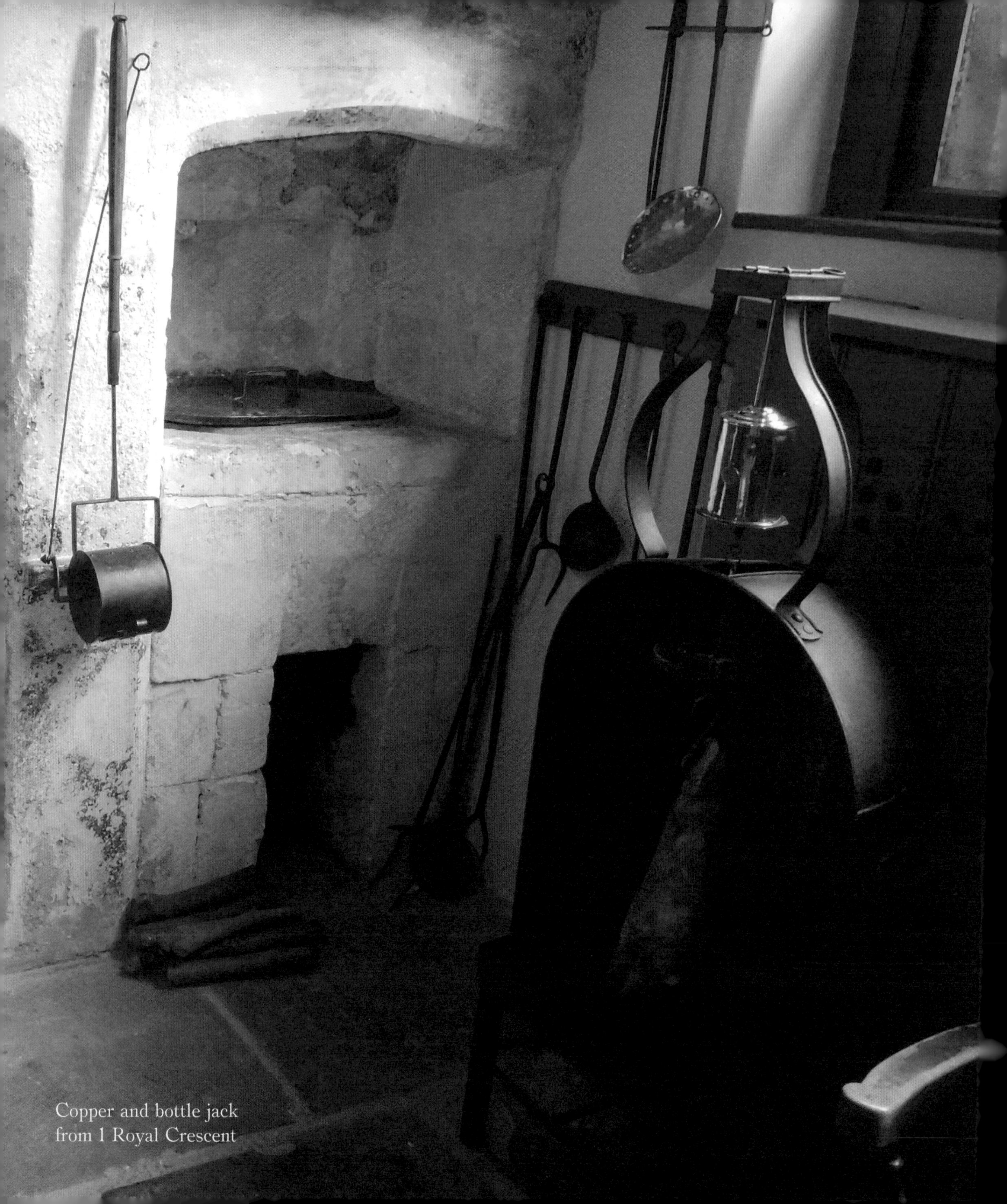

Copper and bottle jack
from 1 Royal Crescent

Meat.

'A beef-steak house is a most excellent place to dine at. You come in there to a warm comfortable large room, where a number of people are sitting at table. You take whatever place you find empty; call for what you like; which you get & well & cleverly drest. You may either chat or not as you like. Nobody minds you; & you pay very reasonably. My dinner, beef, bread & beer & waiter (tip) was only one shilling.'

James Boswell. 1762-3. 'London Journal'.

Beef was seen as the iconic British meat, cooked on a spit in front of a coal fire, banked up in a large cast iron grate.

Steak was so popular that it was cooked in situ in the House of Commons: *'Three successive beef-steaks were broiled under our eyes, over a clear strong fire, incessantly turned, and served good and hot, tender, delicate, and juicy. This is a national dish, rarely good; but under this national roof it proved excellent.'* (1815. Louis Simond. 'An American in Regency England')

Cooked meat was available from 'cook shops', a form of take-away, with various kinds of meat on spits, served with bread. Frances Burney's heroine, Cecilia, said that: *'we eat nothing but cold meat from the cook shops'.* (1782. 'Cecilia') These shops would deliver steak to people in prison, and when Roderick Random visited his friend in the Marshalsea (debtors' prison) they *'dined together on boiled beef and greens, brought from a cook's shop in the neighbourhood'.* They even had a bottle of wine to go with the meal. (1748. Tobias Smollett)

The wealthy provided feasts for the local people on special occasions, and Humphrey Clinker *'ordered some bullocks to be killed, and some hogsheads of ale to be brought from the neighbouring village, to regale these honest people who had not enjoyed such a holiday for many years before'.* (1771. Tobias Smollett)

Parson Woodforde provided lavish feasts for his workers, but in his private life he was experimental in eating different types of meat. Many employed the 'nose to tail' policy that is highly rated today, but he found some meats to be unpalatable: *'I dined .... upon a roasted Tongue and Udder....N.B. I shall not dine on a roasted Tongue and Udder again very soon.'* (1985. 'A Country Parson: James Woodforde's Diary. 1759-1802.')

Virtually no homes had refrigeration until the 19th century, so larders were vital to store meat in a cool environment. Of course not all houses had the space for larders, and town houses would use a 'hanging safe'.

Large houses had game larders and at Uppark in West Sussex, Humphrey Repton designed one with circular hanging racks: *'The game may be so disposed that the windows may all be left to a certain degree unencumbered.'* (from a note in the larder)

It was not uncommon for guests to be taken to view a larder's impressive contents and Caroline Powys visited one that contained *'three brace of pheasants, eight hares, six brace whistling plovers, twelve couple woodcocks, ten brace partridges, a peafowl, two guinea-fowls, snipes and larks without number.'* (1756 – 1808')

6   Meat

Bacon Pudding.

Wiltshire was famous for its method of dry curing bacon, as it was on the route the pig drovers took between Bristol and Hereford.

Robert Smith. 1723. 'Court Cookery.'

A Quart of Cream, and boil it, with a handful of Sugar, and a little Butter; the Yolks of eight Eggs, and three Whites, beat together, with three spoonfuls of Flower, and two spoonfuls of Cream; when the Cream boils, put in the Eggs, stirring it till it comes to be thick, and put it in a Dish, and let it cool; then beat a Piece of fat Bacon in a Stone Mortar till it comes to be like Lard, take out all the Strings from it, and put your Cream to it little by little till it's well mixed; then put some Puff-Paste round the Brim of your Dish, and a thin Leaf at Bottom, and pour it into the Dish. Do the Top Chequerwise with Puff-Paste, and let it bake half an Hour.

Ingredients

(I have divided the quantities approximately by a quarter)

500ml double cream

30g sugar

40g butter

2 egg yolks

2 eggs

Salt and pepper

2 teaspoons of flour

400g streaky bacon

Puff pastry

A little beaten egg

Method

1. Warm the cream with the sugar and butter in a saucepan.

2. Whisk the eggs and egg yolks gently in a bowl with the flour and a little salt and pepper, until there are no lumps.

3. Add the eggs to the cream mixture and stir to thicken over a low heat

4. Fry the bacon until very crisp then roughly chop and drain on kitchen paper.

5. Add the bacon to the cream mixture then allow to cool.

6. Roll out the puff pastry very thin and use it to line a buttered flan dish with a removable base (about 24cm.) Keep the trimmings of the pastry.

7. Pour the bacon and cream mixture into the pastry case.

8. Roll out the pastry trimmings and cut into strips. Arrange these in a criss-cross design over the top of the flan. Brush with beaten egg.

9. Bake at 200°c, gas 6, for 30 minutes, until the top is golden and crisp.

Note: this is like a sweet quiche without any cheese. I fried the bacon instead of blending it, as I prefer to have crunchy bits in the sauce.

Beef Collops.

The word 'collop' comes from the French 'escalope', which is a slice of meat.

Hannah Glasse. 1747. 'The Art of Cookery Made Plain and Easy.'

Take some rump steaks, or tender piece cut like Scotch collops, only larger, hack them a little with a knife, and flour them; put a little butter in a stew-pan, and melt it, then put in your collops, and fry them quick for about two minutes: put in a pint of gravy, a little butter rolled in flour, season with pepper and salt: cut four pickled cucumbers in thin slices, half a walnut, and a few capers, a little onion shred very fine; stew them five minutes, then put them into a hot dish, and send them to table. You may put half a glass of white wine into it.

Ingredients

350g rump steak

1 tablespoon of flour

Salt and pepper

20g butter

1 onion sliced finely

150ml stock

50ml white wine

10g flour

1 tablespoon of pickled cucumbers or gherkins, chopped

1 pickled walnut, chopped

1 tablespoon of capers, chopped

Method

1. Use the blunt side of a knife to make cuts into the steak so that it marks the surface in a criss-cross pattern on both sides.

2. Spread the flour on a plate with salt and pepper and use this to coat the steak on both sides

3. Heat the butter in a frying pan then fry the steak over a high heat for a couple of minutes on each side.

4. Remove the steak from the pan and keep warm.

5. Add the onion to the pan and fry for a few minutes until softened.

6. Stir in the flour then add the stock and wine. Stir to thicken then add the gherkins, pickled walnut and capers.

7. Cook for 5 minutes then return the steak to the pan and cook for a further 5 minutes.

Note: I like to fry the onion as this improves the flavour.

Slices of Beef
with Clear Gravy and Rocombole.

William Verral. 1759. 'A Complete System of Cookery.'

A pound of meat is enough for this dish; cut it into bits about an inch thick, and flat it down with your knife or a light cleaver; it is better than slicing; make it very thin and jagg it with the back of your knife cross and cross, rub a large stewpan with butter, a little green onion and parsley minced, fry your beef briskly for two or three minutes, tossing it that it may be done on both sides, take it out into a small stewpan, and pour in a ladle of nice gravy, a little pepper, salt, a morsel of shallot and parsley, boil it but a moment; when dinner is ready squeeze in a lemon or orange, and send it to table.
The inside fillets of loins or mutton or pork is done in the same manner; and though they seem but trifling matters, yet if care is taken to make them very thin, and nicely fry'd, and not boiled too much afterwards, they are good and pretty dishes.

Ingredients

450g rump or sirloin steak

6 spring onions, finely chopped ('rocambole' is a kind of garlic or shallot)

2 tablespoons of parsley, finely chopped

40g butter

100ml stock

Salt and pepper

2 shallots, sliced

Juice of a lemon or orange

Method

1. Use the blunt side of a knife to mark the surface in a criss-cross pattern on both sides then season with salt and pepper.

2. Mix the spring onions and parsley then coat both sides of the steak in this mixture (this works better than putting it in the pan as suggested in the original recipe).

3. Heat half the butter in a frying pan then add the steak and cook over a high heat until seared on both sides.

4. Remove the steak from the pan and keep it warm.

5. Turn down the heat and put the rest of the butter in the pan and fry the shallots until golden. (You need this second addition of butter as otherwise the mixture will be too dry.) Add the stock and cook for a couple of minutes then add the lemon or orange juice and check the seasoning.

Note: William Verral's recipe for gravy involves 3-4 pounds of meat, a slice of raw ham and a little fat bacon, 2-3 onions, carrots, parsley, cooked with a little broth until brown. This is rather expensive so I just use a good beef or chicken stock.

Chicken Curry.

English involvement in India led to an interest in spiced food, which resulted in the opening of a number of curry houses in London.

Hannah Glasse wrote the first recipe for curry in England in 1747. It was very simple and only used pepper and coriander seeds, with rice added during the cooking. A later edition of her book added ginger and turmeric, and the rice was served separately.

William Kitchiner. 1817. ' The Cook's Oracle and Housekeeper's Manual.'

Cut fowls or rabbits into joints, and wash them clean: put two ounces of butter into a stew-pan; when it is melted, put in the meat, and two middling-sized onions sliced, let them be over a smart fire till they are of a light brown, then put in half a pint of broth; let it simmer twenty minutes.

Put in a basin one or two table-spoonfuls of curry powder, a tea-spoonful of flour, and a tea-spoonful of salt; mix it smooth with a little cold water, put it into the stew-pan, and shake it well about till it boils: let it simmer twenty minutes longer; then take out the meat, and rub the sauce through a tamis or sieve: add to it two table spoonfuls of cream or milk; give it a boil up; then pour it into a dish, lay the meat over it: send up the rice in a separate dish.

Observation._Curry is made also with sweetbreads, breast of veal, veal cutlets, lamb, mutton or pork chops, lobster, turbot, soles, eels, oysters, &c.: prepared as above.

Ingredients

2 tablespoons curry powder (see section on 'Preserves' for Kitchiner's recipe)

1 teaspoon of flour

1 teaspoon of salt

8 chicken thighs

60g butter

2 red onions, sliced

300ml stock

2 tablespoons of cream

Method

1. Mix the curry powder with the flour and salt in a large bowl. Add the chicken thighs and mix to coat them thoroughly.

2. Melt the butter in a large frying pan. Add the chicken and cook over a medium to high flame until golden on all sides. Remove the chicken to a casserole dish. Fry the onions in the same pan until golden, then add them to the casserole.

3. Pour the stock and cream into the pan and stir around, then pour this over the chicken and onions. Cook gently for about 40 minutes until tender.

4. Serve with rice.

Note: coating the chicken in the spices seems to produce a better result than mixing the spices to a paste with water as in the original recipe. I also prefer to cook the chicken and onion separately to make sure both have the chance to caramelise. I don't think it is necessary to blend the sauce, but you can if you want a smoother result. This is also good made with 2 rabbits (jointed), or 400g lamb steaks (cut up roughly).

Chicken Salad

('To make a Sallet of a cold Capon, or Pullet').

Frederick Nutt. 1809. 'The Imperial and Royal Cookbook.'

Cut the Breast of a Capon, or Pullet roasted, in as thin slices as you can; put in Vinegar, and a little Sugar, if you please; then mince together a Handful of Capers, a little long Grass, or Tarragon, and half a dozen Anchovies; when these are minced, but not too small, strew all on your Sallet; garnish with Oranges, Lemons, or Barberries, and serve it up with a little Salt.

Ingredients

400g chicken breast, cut into thin strips and seasoned with salt and pepper

A little oil

1 orange

1 tablespoon of vinegar

1 teaspoon of sugar

1 tablespoon of capers, chopped

1 tablespoon of chives, or a teaspoon of tarragon, chopped

6 anchovies, cut up roughly

Lettuce leaves

A little salt (preferably sea salt flakes)

Method

1. Brush a griddle or pan with the oil and fry the chicken strips over a high heat until golden.

2. Cut the orange vertically into segments, discarding the membrane. Retain any juice.

3. Mix the vinegar, sugar and retained orange juice and pour over the chicken while still warm

4. Add the capers, herbs and anchovies and taste to check the seasoning

5. Serve on a bed of lettuce.

6. Garnish with the orange segments and a sprinkle of salt

Note: William Kitchiner wrote that: *'Salad is a very compound dish with our neighbours the French, who always add to the mixture, black pepper, and sometimes savoury spice.* (1817. 'The Cook's Oracle.')

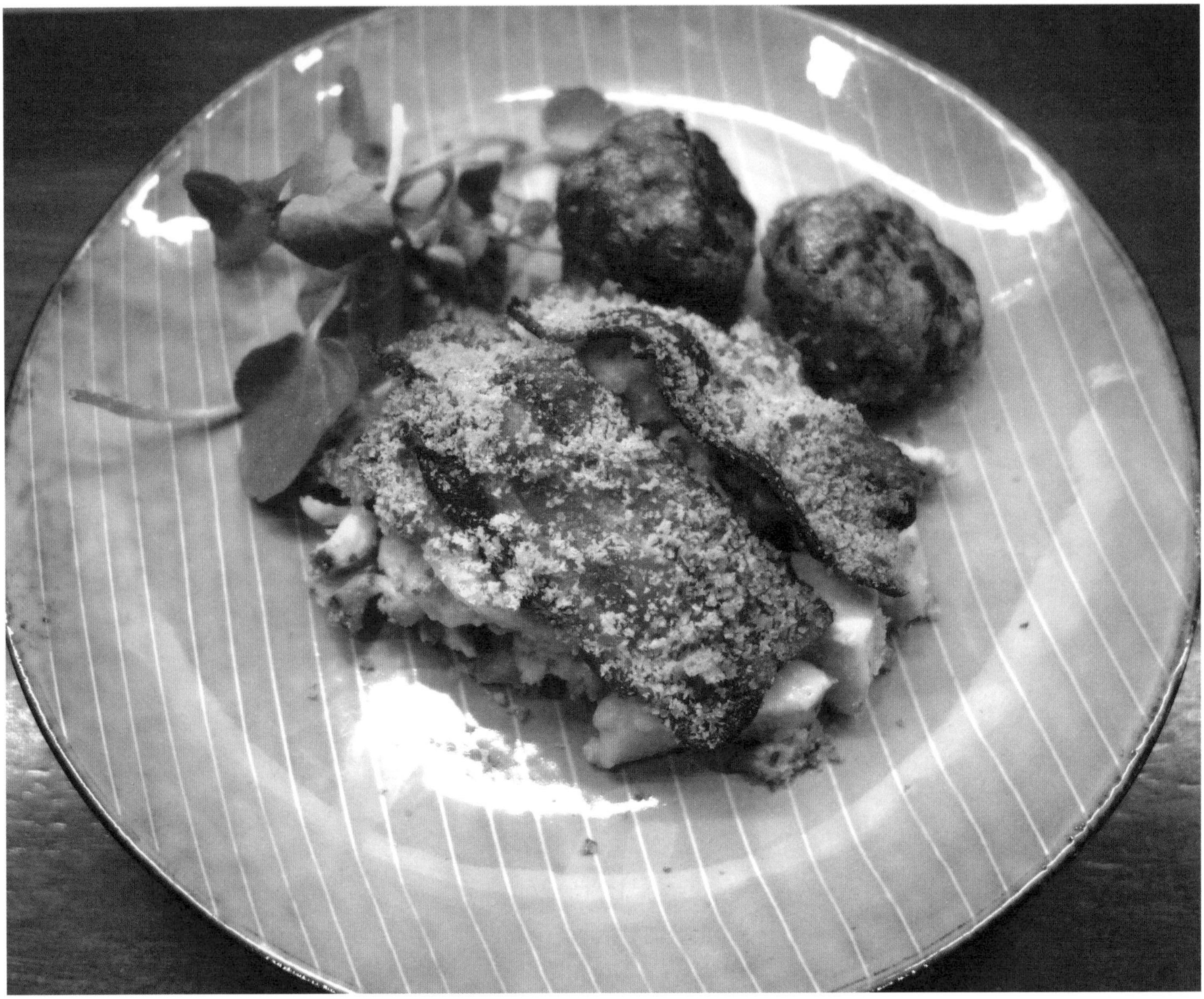

Chicken Surprise.

Poultry yards were increasing in popularity and poultry maids were employed specifically for their care. At Shugborough in Staffordshire, Sir John Soane designed a poultry yard that aimed to be both attractive and functional.

A 'mazarine' is an oval pierced plate, which is placed in a dish when serving fish or meat.

Ingredients

1 chicken

15g butter

1 tablespoon of flour

120ml cream

Salt and pepper

6 rashers of streaky bacon

30g freshly made breadcrumbs

Forcemeat (Farley's recipe):

50g streaky bacon, roughly chopped

75g breadcrumbs

3 tablespoons of fresh herbs like marjoram, thyme, parsley

1 egg

Salt and pepper

Sauce:

50ml stock

20g butter

Juice of half a lemon

John Farley. 1792. 'The London Art of Cookery.'

One large fowl will do for a small dish. Roast it, and take the lean from the bones; cut it into thin slices, about an inch long, and toss it up with six or seven spoonsful of cream, and a piece of butter, as big as a walnut, rolled in flour. Boil it up, and set it to cool. Then put six or seven thin slices of bacon round it, place them in a pattypan, and put some forcemeat on each side. Work them up into the form of a French roll, with a raw egg, leaving a hollow place in the middle. Put in your fowl, and cover them with some of the same forcemeat, rubbing them smooth with a raw egg. Make them of the height and bigness of a French roll, and throw a little fine grated bread over them. Bake them three quarters, or an hour, in a gentle oven, or under a baking cover, till they come to a fine brown, and place them on your mazarine, that they may not touch one another; but place them so that they may not fall flat in the baking; or you may form them on your table with a broad kitchen knife, and place them on the thing you intend to bake them on. You may put the leg of a chicken into one of the loaves you in tend for the middle. Let your sauce be gravy, thickened with butter, and a little juice of a lemon.

Method

1. Roast the chicken. Allow it to cool then pull off the meat and slice finely.

2. Melt the butter in a pan and add the flour. Cook gently then add the cream. Stir well then add the chicken and seasoning. Allow to cool.

3. Lay out the bacon in a buttered ovenproof dish then put the chicken mixture in a sausage shape down the centre of the bacon. Wrap the bacon round the chicken then sprinkle over the breadcrumbs.

4. To make the forcemeat, blend the breadcrumbs with the bacon, seasoning and herbs then add the egg to bind it. Fry a little of the mixture until golden, then taste it to check the seasoning. Form the forcemeat into 8-10 small balls and place them around the chicken in the dish. Bake at 180°c, gas 4, for 45 minutes.

5. To make the sauce, heat the stock, butter and lemon juice in a pan.

To Hash Ducks.

This is an unusual dish, as we are not used to cooked cucumber. It is surprisingly good.

Ingredients

Half a cucumber sliced, but not too finely (I prefer to cut the cucumber in half and scrape out the seeds. This makes it less watery.)

1 onion, sliced

50ml cider vinegar

1 teaspoon of salt

2 duck breasts (or you can use the meat that is left over from a roast duck)

Salt and pepper

A slice of gammon (about 50g)

100ml stock ('cullis' was a strong meat stock)

20g butter mixed with 10g flour

Collingwood and Woollams. 1792. 'The Universal Cook.'

Having roasted two ducks till they be nearly three parts done, take them up, and let them stand to cool. Then cut the breast into thin slices, and take care of the gravy. The legs will serve for another dish, which you may dress by wrapping them in a caul with a good forcemeat, and serve them up with cullis sauce. For the fillets, cut cucumbers, and marinade them about an hour, with a little vinegar, salt, and an onion sliced. Then take out the onion, squeeze the cucumbers in a cloth, and put them into a stewpan with a bit of butter, a slice of ham, a little broth, flour, and veal gravy. Boil it slowly, skim it well, take out the ham, and put the meat to it to warm, without boiling. You may do the same with chopped truffles, or mushrooms, or any thing else in season. You may hash a cold roasted duck in this manner.

Method

1. Marinate the cucumber with the onion in the vinegar and salt for about an hour. Rinse and drain.

2. Season the duck breasts then fry them skin side down in a non-stick pan for 10 minutes. Turn them and cook for another 10 minutes then remove them and keep them warm.

3. Put the cucumber in a pan with the gammon and stock. Add the butter mixed with the flour. Heat gently until the sauce has thickened then lift out the gammon.

4. Slice the duck breast, and add this with its juices to the pan. Stir gently until it is hot. I like to slice the gammon finely and serve it alongside the duck, even though this is not part of the original recipe. It seems a pity to waste it.

Note: A 'cullis' is a strong broth or stock, used as the basis for sauces.

Here I have focused on the main part of the recipe that uses the duck breast and have not included the part that uses the legs.

To Hash Mutton.

Mutton was more readily available in Georgian times than it is now. If you can find mutton, allow longer for it to cook.

Tobias Smollett's character Roderick Random was enthusiastic about mutton hash as a *'hearty supper'*. (1748.) George 3rd was particularly fond of Portland mutton, which he used to eat when he stayed in Weymouth. Portland sheep are valued for their wool and milk so are kept for longer before slaughter, which improves the flavour.

Ingredients

2 onions, finely sliced

40g butter

600g lamb steaks, trimmed and thinly sliced (you can use the trimmings to make a stock, as in the recipe above)

A couple of heaped teaspoons of flour, seasoned with salt and pepper

150ml stock (made as above)

50ml red wine

20g capers, rinsed and chopped

20g gherkins, chopped

2 tablespoons of sweet herbs such as chives, parsley, basil or coriander, chopped finely

30g pickled walnuts, chopped, and a tablespoon of their vinegar

Salt and pepper

Fingers of fried bread (sippets)

Francis Collingwood and John Woollams. 1792. 'The Universal Cook.'

Having cut your mutton into small pieces, and as thin as you can, strew a little flour over it, and put it into some gravy, in which sweet herbs, onion, pepper, and salt, have been boiled, and strained. Put in a piece of butter rolled in flour, a little salt, a shallot cut fine, a few capers and gerkins finely chopped, and a glass of red wine, or walnut pickles, if you like it. Toss all together for a minute or two, and have ready some bread toasted and cut into thin sippets; lay these round the dish, and pour in your hash. Garnish with pickles and horse-radish and send it up to table.

Method

1. Fry the onions in half the butter and then transfer them to an ovenproof dish with a lid.

2. Dip the lamb strips in the seasoned flour then fry them over a high flame in the same pan, with the rest of the butter, until browned (you may need to do this in batches). Put these in the dish with the onions.

3. Add the stock to the pan and stir to collect the bits from the meat and onions.

4. Add the wine, capers, gherkins, herbs, walnuts and the vinegar, then pour the mixture over the lamb and onions in the ovenproof dish.

5. Cover and cook in the oven at 180°c, gas 4, for 40 – 50 minutes, until the lamb is tender.

6. Taste to check the seasoning.

7. Serve with fried bread (sippets) around the outside of the dish.

Note: The authors recommended that this dish should be served with pickles (see recipes for pickled mushrooms and pickled red cabbage in the 'Preserves' section)

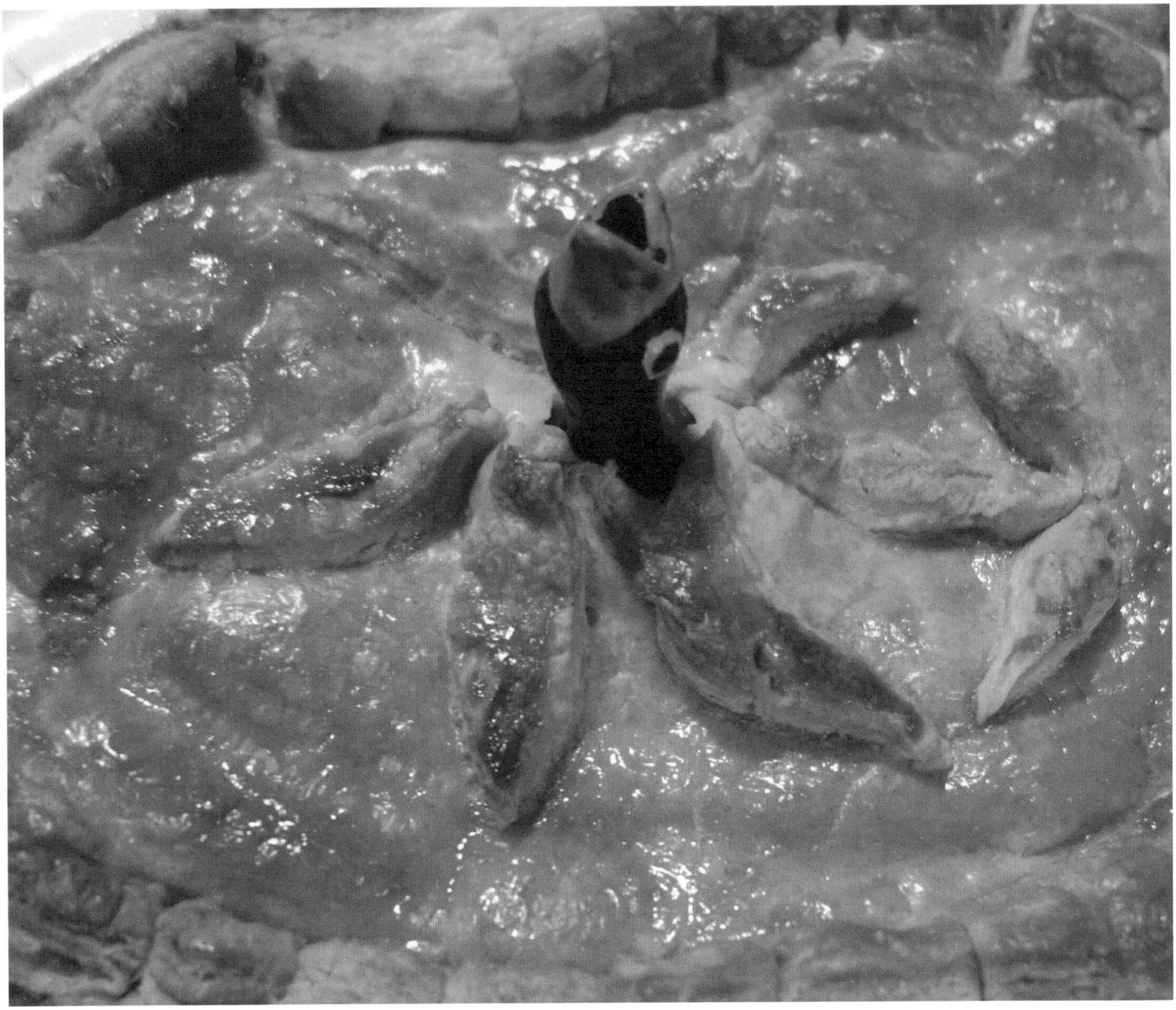

A Sweet Lamb Pie.

Robert Smith. 1723. 'Court Cookery.'

Cut an Hind Quarter of Lamb into thin slices; season it with Mace, Nutmeg, Cinnamon, and Salt, and lay it in the Pie; mix with it half a Pound of Raisins of the Sun stoned, half a Pound of Currans, two or three Potatoes boiled, blanched, and sliced, or an Artichoke-bottom, with Prunelloes and Damsins, Goose-berries and Grapes, Citron and Lemon Chips, a little Sugar; and lay on Butter, and close the Pie. When bak'd, put a sweet Caudle made thus: Take Sack, White- wine, and a like Quantity of Verjuice and Sugar; boil it, and brew it with three Eggs. When the Pie is bak'd, pour it in at the Funnel, and shake it together.

Ingredients

1 tablespoon of oil

20g butter

500g lamb steaks, trimmed and sliced finely

1 teaspoon of ground mace

Some grated nutmeg

1 teaspoon of cinnamon

1 teaspoon of salt

1 teaspoon of sugar

200ml stock

100ml white wine

1 tablespoon of verjuice or the juice of 1 lemon

50ml sherry (previously known as sack)

3 eggs, beaten

50g sultanas, currants or prunes, roughly chopped

200g plums, stones removed and chopped roughly

Zest of a lemon, sliced finely

100 - 150g artichoke hearts, sliced

400g potatoes, peeled, cooked then sliced

Puff pastry

Method

1. Heat the oil and butter in a frying pan and add the lamb. Cook over a high heat until browned on both sides (this caramelises it, improving the flavour).

2. Add the mace, nutmeg, cinnamon, sugar and salt then stir.

3. Add the stock, the wine and verjuice or lemon juice and simmer for about an hour until the lamb is tender. Remove from the heat then add the sherry and most of the beaten eggs. Stir as the mixture thickens (save a little of the egg to brush the pastry).

4. Add the sultanas, currants or prunes, plums and lemon zest and mix well.

5. Put the artichoke hearts in your pie dish then half of the meat mixture. Cover this with the potatoes and season with some salt and pepper. Cover this with the other half of the meat mixture. Allow to cool then chill in the fridge for at least half an hour.

6. When it is cold, cover the dish with a layer of puff pastry, brush with the remaining beaten egg, then chill again.

7. Heat the oven to 200°c, gas 6 then put in the pie. Cook for 25-30 minutes.

Note: a caudle is a hot, thick alcoholic drink. I added the caudle ingredients to the pie filling, which is simpler than pouring it in at the end.

I have left out the gooseberries and the grapes to make it more practical, and also more appealing to modern tastes. Of course you can add them if you like.

At Wimpole Hall in Cambridgeshire, both white and black grapes were grown in a glass-house designed by John Soane.

Pigeons à la Duxelle.

Dovecotes or pigeon houses were often grand structures, associated with privilege. Many less affluent people aspired to such grandeur and Tobias Smollett's character Matt Bramble described how his makeshift pigeon house: *'made an agreeable figure in my yard;'* (1771. 'Humphrey Clinker.')

Ingredients

100g streaky bacon, chopped

2 shallots, finely chopped

200g mushrooms, chopped

Salt and pepper

A little ground nutmeg

1 teaspoon of thyme leaves

6-8 spring onions, sliced

8 pigeon breasts (this is far simpler to prepare and to eat than using whole pigeons)

300ml chicken stock

Juice and zest of 2 oranges or lemons

1 tablespoon of basil leaves, roughly chopped

1 tablespoon of parsley leaves, chopped

8 slices of ham, cut very thin

A little chopped parsley

Francis Collingwood and John Woollams. 1792. 'The Universal Cook.'

Take four or five pigeons, cut off their feet and pinions, and split them down the breast; then take out the livers, and flatten them with a cleaver. Make a hot marinade of some scraped bacon, seasoned with a mushroom or two, green onions, pepper, salt, thyme, parsley, and a little nutmeg. Fry all for a few minutes, and let the pigeons be heated through in it, and let them remain till you put them upon your gridiron. Take a thin slice of ham for each pigeon, and put them with the ham always at top; that is, when you turn your pigeons, turn your ham upon them. For your sauce, take a ladle of gravy, some sweet basil, a little thyme, parsley, and shallot, minced very fine, and a few slices of mushrooms, boiled all together a few minutes. Dish them up with their breast downwards, let your ham continue upon them, and pour your sauce over them, with the juice of an orange or lemon.

Method

1. Fry the bacon in a pan for 5 minutes, until starting to change colour.

2. Add the shallots and fry for 5 - 10 minutes, until translucent (if there is not enough fat from the bacon, then add a little butter at this stage).

3. Add the mushrooms, salt, pepper, nutmeg, thyme and spring onions. Fry for 5 minutes then add the seasoned pigeon breasts. Sear on each side then remove them and keep them warm.

4. Add the stock and orange or lemon juice and zest to the pan and boil for 10 minutes to reduce the liquid. Add the basil and parsley.

5. Wrap each pigeon breast in a slice of ham then sear on a hot griddle until golden brown on both sides.

6. Serve the pigeon breasts on a bed of the sauce, with a little parsley sprinkled over.

Venison Semey.

During the eighteenth century most of the great houses had private deer parks, demonstrating their wealth. The grounds at Kedleston Hall in Derbyshire were designed by Robert Adam and included a deer park. James Boswell was enthusiastic in his description of the *'extensive park, with the finest verdure, covered with deer, and cattle, and sheep.'* (James Boswell. 'The Life of Samuel Johnson'. 1791)

Venison was a symbol of the highest social status and there were strict laws to prevent poaching, which could be punished by death.

Robert Smith. 1723. 'Court Cookery.'

Boil your Venison till it is fit to be eaten, make a sweet Paste of brown Loaf grated small, and a candied Orange-peel, minced fine, a Pound and a half, or two Pound of Sugar, a Pint of White-wine, seasoned with Nutmeg, Mace and Salt; mix it all well together with your Hand, and put it about your Venison, and bake it an Hour; and when you serve it up, put into the Dish White-wine boil'd with Spice and Sugar, and sift Sugar over it.

Ingredients

700 - 750g venison, prepared weight, cut into smallish chunks

2 teaspoons of ground mace

2 teaspoons of ground nutmeg

Salt and pepper

2-3 tablespoons of oil

400ml stock

50g candied orange, chopped (see recipe in the 'preserves' section), or the zest of an orange mixed with 25g sugar.

25g sugar (greatly reduced quantity)

50ml white wine

125g freshly made brown breadcrumbs (stale or sourdough bread is best as you don't want the mixture to be too soft)

Method

1. Season the venison with half the mace and nutmeg, and some salt and pepper.

2. Fry the venison in the oil over a high heat until browned. You will need to fry the meat in batches or it will not caramelise well. As you cook the meat, transfer it to an ovenproof dish. (I fried the venison instead of boiling it as in the original recipe, as this improves the flavour)

3. Pour the stock into the frying pan and stir it around to collect up all of the meaty flavours then pour it over the venison. Cook in the oven at 160°c, gas 3, for an hour.

4. Mix the candied orange or zest, sugar, wine, breadcrumbs, the remaining mace and nutmeg, and season. Scatter this over the venison.

5. Cover with a lid or foil, and cook in the oven at 160°c, gas 3, for half an hour. Remove the lid and cook for another half hour

Note: the original version of this dish would be far too sweet for modern tastes so I have reduced the quantity of sugar accordingly. I omitted the sauce mentioned at the end of the original recipe, as the dish already has plenty of liquid.

This recipe uses venison in a style that seems intended to have a Russian influence: 'Semey' was a Russian fort in eastern Kazakhstan, near Siberia.

Fishing pavillion at Kedlestone Hall, Derbyshire
© Reproduced by kind permission of the National Trust

Fish.

'A fishing pole is a stick with a hook at one end and a fool on the other.'

Samuel Johnson

The great houses usually had a river or a lake stocked with fish. At Kedlestone Hall in Derbyshire, a specially designed pavilion was built on the upper lake so that the Curzon family could fish from the window, protected from the elements.

The diarist Caroline Powys described a trip to Stokes Bay to watch the fishermen bring in the shrimp. She also went to Ryde where she ate *'sand-eels, the nicest little things I ever tasted, like whitebait',* as well as lobster, crab and mackerel. She was fascinated by the sheds where herring were dried: *'When they have hung out of doors two days they are wash'd in tubs of brine, then brought to an inner house to the gang of women, twelve in a gang, who spit them on sticks, which hang from the ceiling to the floor, on cross-band beams from the top, about 40 or 50 feet high, then fires are made under them by sticks of 4 feet long, the size according to Act of Parliament, and when dry'd put into barrels.' (1756-1808')*

Storage of fish was an important issue. Wealthy families had ice houses for the ice collected from their lakes in winter (there was a mini ice age at the time). As demand increased, larger ice houses were built in towns. Eventually it became necessary to import ice from America, Greenland and Norway to satisfy the needs of the fishing industry. William Kitchiner warned against fish that had been kept too long on the boats, which was sold off at a reduced price: *'it frequently happens that they are at sea*

perhaps a fortnight, when the greater part of the fish is perished... This accounts for the very low prices at which the itinerant fishmongers cry their "delicate salmon," "dainty fresh salmon..." (1817. 'The Cook's Oracle.')

A fresher option was the thriving fishing industry on the Thames; whitebait could be caught at Blackwall Reach and were regularly served for suppers in the taverns of Greenwich.

Fish was popular throughout the eateries of London, such as Simpsons Tavern, a well known 'ordinary' (a restaurant with a fixed price menu), which opened in 1723 in Bell Alley, Billingsgate, London, next to the market. The stallholders would take fish along and it would be cooked for their lunch.

Oysters were considered to be a delicious snack before dinner: *'a round of toast and butter, and a few oysters, fresh-opened, by way of a damper before dinner.'* (Frances Burney. 1782. 'Cecilia.') However, human waste often polluted the oyster beds, leading to the spread of diseases such as typhoid. Tobias Smollett described how they were *'kept in slime-pits, occasionally overflowed by the sea; and that green colour, so much admired by the voluptuaries of this metropolis, is occasioned by the vitriolic scum, which rises on the surface of the stagnant and stinking water.'* (1771. 'Humphrey Clinker.') I assume that few of the diners were aware of these unpleasant facts.

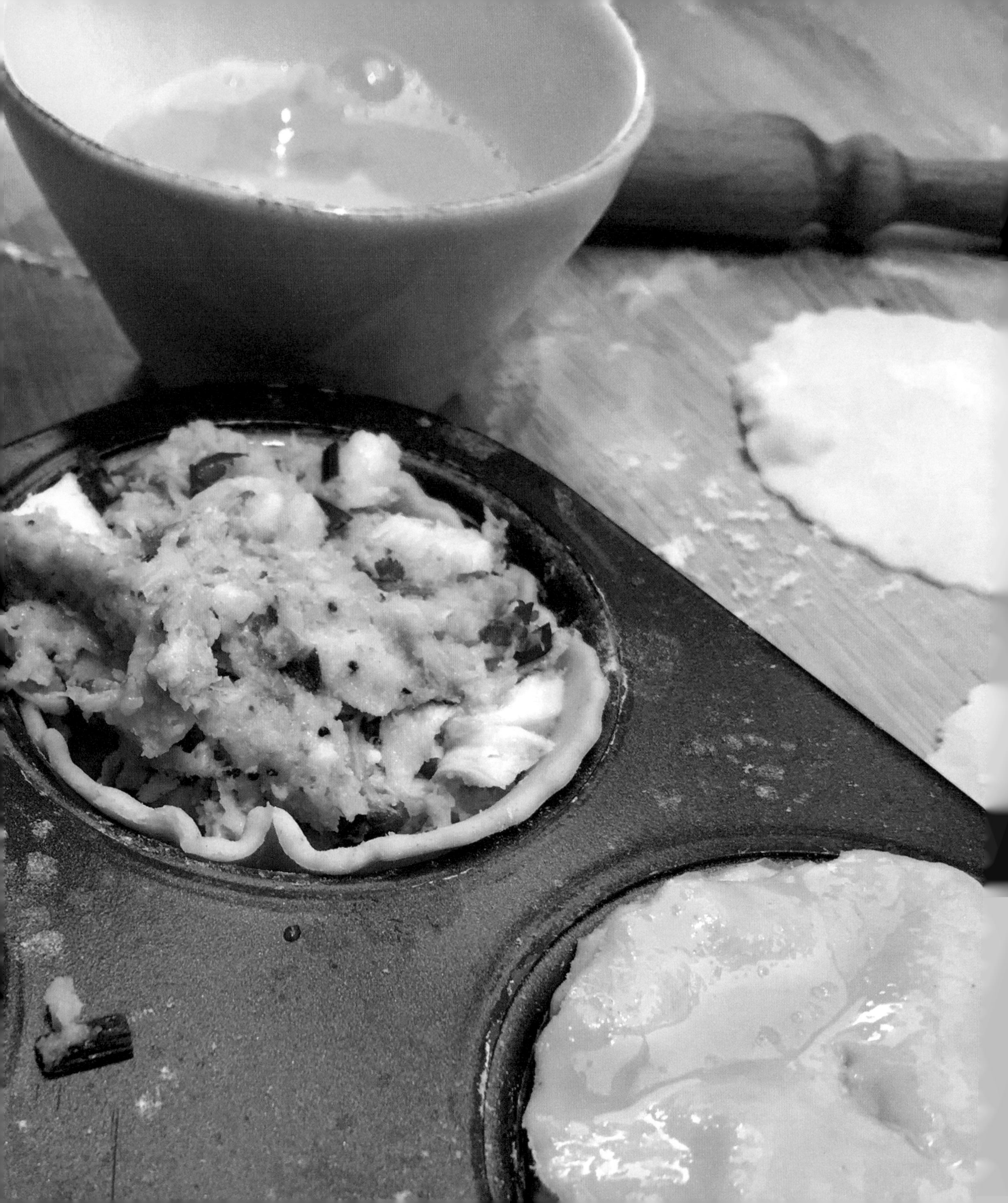

Fish Patties.

Richard Briggs. 1788. 'The English Art of Cookery.'

Take about a pound of any kind of fresh fish, boil it and pick the meat from the bones, beat it well in a mortar, with half a pound of bread-crumbs, some parsley and lemon-peel shred fine, season it with beaten mace, pepper and salt; put in a quarter of a pound of fresh butter, mix it up with the yolk of an egg, butter your patty-pans, lay in a thin sheet of puff-paste, roll some of the force-meat round, and put in, put a cover of puff-paste over with the yolk of an egg, and bake them of a gold colour.

Ingredients

500-600g fillets of cod or hake

100ml white wine

100g butter

Salt and pepper

225g breadcrumbs

Zest of half a lemon

4 tablespoons of parsley leaves, chopped

1 teaspoon of ground mace

1 egg yolk

Puff pastry

A little beaten egg

Method

1. Cook the fish with the wine, butter, salt and pepper for about 10 minutes, turning once, until it starts to flake. Remove any skin and bones.

2. Beat together the breadcrumbs, lemon zest, parsley, mace and egg yolk. Add the fish and the cooking liquid and season with salt and pepper. This is a kind of 'forcemeat' or stuffing.

3. Roll out half the pastry very thin and cut circles. Butter your bun tins and dust them with flour then put in the pastry circles.

4. Fill the pastry cases with the fish mixture.

5. Roll out the remaining pastry and cut into smaller circles that will fit on top of your patties. Make a cut in the top of each and brush with beaten egg. Chill in the fridge for at least half an hour.

6. Bake for 25 minutes at 180°c, gas 4, until golden brown.

Note: this makes about 12 individual 'patties'. I cooked the fish in wine to improve the flavour and reduced the breadcrumbs, to make the patties lighter.

To Broil Haddocks.

Sarah Martin. 1795. 'The New Experienced English-Housekeeper.'

Clean them as for boiling (take out the gills), and put a pudding in their bellies; lay them in a dripping-pan and rub them with yolk of egg, strew over them bread crumbs, dredge them with flour, then set them before a brisk fire, baste them and make them a good brown on both sides; garnish and serve them up with cockle or anchovy sauce.

Ingredients

400g haddock fillet

1 carrot

1 stick of celery

1 shallot

Herbs

2-3 tablespoons flour, seasoned with salt and pepper

1 egg, beaten

50g fresh breadcrumbs

A little butter for frying

Forcemeat or 'pudding' (see Sarah Martin's recipe on following page)

Anchovy sauce (see Sarah Martin's recipe on following page)

Method

1. First make the forcemeat or 'pudding' – see recipe on facing page.

2. Remove the skin from the fish then trim the fillets. Put the skin and trimmings into a pan with water and a carrot, a stick of celery, a shallot and whatever herbs you have. Boil this for about 30 minutes and use it to make fish stock for the anchovy sauce (see recipe on facing page).

3. Cut the haddock into pieces (the size depends on your taste) then dip them first into the seasoned flour, then the egg, and finally in the breadcrumbs.

4. Heat some butter in a pan and fry the haddock in batches over a medium flame, until it is golden on both sides.

5. Serve with the forcemeat balls and anchovy sauce.

Note: few people today are likely to cook a whole haddock, so the forcemeat is best fried as balls rather than as a stuffing for the fish, as suggested in the original recipe.

Forcemeat.

Ingredients

100g breadcrumbs

100g butter, melted (to replace the beef suet)

1 egg, beaten

1-2 anchovy fillets

Half a lemon, zest and juice

1 teaspoon of mace

1 teaspoon of nutmeg

1 teaspoon of cayenne

1 teaspoon of thyme leaves

1 tablespoon of marjoram leaves, picked from the stem and chopped

Sarah Martin. 1795. 'The New Experienced English-Housekeeper.'

To make a pudding for the belly of stale bread crumbs and beef suet equal quantities, an anchovy, a little lemon peel, beaten mace, nutmeg, chyan pepper, a sprig of thyme, one pot-marjoram and a little lemon juice, mix them up with an egg, and sew it in the belly.

Method

1. Combine all of the ingredients and chill for at least half an hour for the mixture to set.

2. Form into balls and fry briefly in a non-stick pan until golden. Arrange these round the outside of the dish in which you serve the haddock.

Anchovy Sauce.

Ingredients

50g butter

2-3 anchovies, chopped

1 teaspoon of grated nutmeg

2-3 teaspoons of vinegar from a jar of pickled walnuts (or use balsamic vinegar)

150ml stock (preferably beef or lamb, but chicken or fish are also good)

Sarah Martin. 1795. 'The New Experienced English-Housekeeper.'

Melt some good butter, chop two or three anchovies, put them in the butter with grated nutmeg, two or three spoonsful of walnut-catchup, and a little beef or mutton gravy if you have it, then just give it a boil.

Method

1. Melt the butter in a small saucepan then add the rest of the ingredients.

2. Boil until the liquid has reduced by at least half.

Note: 'catchup' was originally a Chinese sauce made from fermented fish. Georgian cooks made their own versions, usually thin and dark in colour, out of vinegar, anchovies and spices. Tomatoes were not added until the 19th century.

Mackerel Caveach.

Francis Collingwood and John Woollams. 1792. 'The Art of Cookery.'

This is made of mackerel, which you must cut into round pieces, and divide into five or six. To six large mackerel, you may take one ounce of beaten pepper, three large nutmegs, a little mace, and a handful of salt. Mix your salt and beaten spice together; then make two or three holes in each piece, and thrust the seasoning into the holes with your finger. Rub each piece all over with the seasoning, fry them brown in sweet oil, and let them stand till they are cold. Put them into a jar, cover them with vinegar, and pour sweet oil over them. They are very delicious, and if well covered, they will keep a long time.

Ingredients

(I have halved the quantities given in the original recipe)

1 teaspoon of ground black pepper

Half a nutmeg, grated finely

1 teaspoon of ground mace

1 teaspoon of salt

3 mackerel, filleted, trimmed and small bones removed

100ml olive oil

100ml cider vinegar or white wine vinegar

Method

1. Combine the pepper, nutmeg, mace and salt.

2. Halve the mackerel fillets and cut into chunks. Coat the fleshy side with the spices, rubbing the mixture in thoroughly.

3. Heat the oil in a frying pan until it is really hot then fry the mackerel, skin-side down, until crisp. Turn them over and fry for a couple of minutes, then place them in a serving dish, skin side down.

4. Add the vinegar to the pan and stir around, then pour this over the mackerel.

5. Serve with thin slices of toast or bread.

Note: this is also good with sardines. These quantities are right for 5-6 sardines.

To Fricassée Prawns.

John Nott. 1723. 'The Cook and Confectioner's Dictionary.'

Take the Meat out of the Shells, put it into a Dish with a Pint of Claret, an Onion slic'd small, a couple of Anchovies, and a Bunch of sweet Herbs; let these stew over a Chafing-dish of Coals with Nutmeg and Ginger; then put them into a Frying-pan with the Yolk of an Egg or two, some Butter and Vinegar; and when they have had a toss or two, serve them up on Sippets.

Ingredients

200ml red or white wine (I think white wine makes the dish look more attractive)

1 shallot or half an onion, finely sliced

2 anchovies

4 tablespoons of the leaves of herbs such as chives, parsley or tarragon, chopped

1 teaspoon of ground nutmeg

A few slices of fresh ginger

20g butter

1 tablespoon of cider vinegar or white wine vinegar

2 large egg yolks

Salt and pepper

500g raw prawns

Sippets – which are strips of fried bread

Method

1. Place the wine in a saucepan with the shallot or onion, anchovies, most of the herbs, nutmeg and ginger. Simmer until reduced by half.

2. Pass the sauce through a sieve into a frying pan and add the butter, vinegar and egg yolks (this is best done off the heat). Return to a very low heat then stir gently as the sauce thickens, and season. Add the prawns and cook until they are starting to turn pink. Check the seasoning.

3. Serve these with a sprinkling of the remaining herbs, and with fingers of fried bread.

Note: a chafing dish was placed on a tripod, to cook dishes gently over charcoal,

Salmon au Court-Bouillon.

Ingredients

(I have greatly reduced the quantities given in the original recipe)

500g piece of filleted salmon

1 teaspoon of ground mace

A pinch of ground cloves

1 teaspoon of ground black pepper

1 teaspoon of salt

Half a nutmeg, grated

Zest of 1 lemon

25g herbs, finely chopped e.g. parsley or dill

100ml white wine

100ml fish stock or water

25ml vinegar (this is less than the proportion originally suggested)

2 teaspoons of creamed horseradish (optional)

50g butter (this is less than the proportion originally suggested)

10g flour

Parsley leaves

Hannah Glasse. 1747. 'The Art of Cookery Made Plain and Easy.'

After having washed and made your salmon very clean, score the side pretty deep, that it may take the seasoning: take a quarter of an ounce of mace, a quarter of an ounce of cloves, a nutmeg, dry them and beat them fine, a quarter of an ounce of black pepper beat fine, and an ounce of salt. Lay the salmon in a napkin, season it well with this spice, cut some lemon peel fine, and parsley, throw all over, and in the notches put about a pound of fresh butter rolled in flour, roll it up tight in the napkin, and bind it about with pack-thread. Put it in a fish-kettle, just big enough to hold it, pour in a quart of white wine, a quart of vinegar, and as much water as will just boil it. Set it over a quick fire, cover it close; when it is enough, which you must judge by the bigness of your salmon, set it over a stove to stew till you are ready. Then have a clean napkin folded in the dish it is to lay it in, out of the napkin it was boiled in on the other napkin. Garnish the dish with a good deal of parsley crisped before the fire.

For sauce have nothing but plain butter in a cup, or horse-radish and vinegar. Serve it up for a first course.

Method

1. Make cuts in the skin of the salmon.

2. Mix the mace, cloves, pepper, salt, nutmeg, lemon zest and herbs. Rub this into the salmon on both sides.

3. Place the salmon in a large, buttered ovenproof dish, skin side up.

4. Combine the wine, fish stock, vinegar and horseradish and pour around the salmon. Cover with foil and bake in the oven at 180°c, gas 4 for 30 minutes.

5. Peel off the skin then turn the salmon over and place on a warm serving dish.

6. Combine the butter and flour and add some salt and pepper

7. Pour the cooking liquid into a pan and add the butter and flour mixture then simmer until the sauce has thickened. Pour over the fish.

8. Garnish with parsley.

Salmon with Sweet Herbs.

Frederick Nutt. 1809. 'The Imperial and Royal Cookbook.'

Mix a piece of butter with some chopped parsley, shalots, sweet herbs, mushrooms, pepper and salt: put some of this in the bottom of the dish you intend to send to table, then some thin slices of salmon upon it, and the remainder of the butter and herbs upon the salmon: strew it over with bread crumbs, then baste it with butter, and bake it in the oven: when it is enough, drain the fat from it, and serve it up with a clear relishing sauce.

Ingredients

500g salmon

75g butter at room temperature

4 shallots, sliced

250-300g mushrooms, sliced

6-8 tablespoons of the leaves of herbs such as parsley, dill or tarragon, chopped

Salt and pepper

50g breadcrumbs

Method

1. Remove the skin from the salmon and cut it into thin slices.

2. Melt 50g butter in a frying pan and add the shallots. Fry until softened then add the mushrooms, herbs and season with salt and pepper. Fry for 5 minutes. (I think frying the vegetables improves the flavour of the dish)

3. Put half of the mixture into an ovenproof dish then place the salmon on top and season. Cover with the rest of the mixture.

4. Sprinkle the breadcrumbs over the top and dot with the remaining butter. Bake at 180°c, gas 4, for 20 minutes.

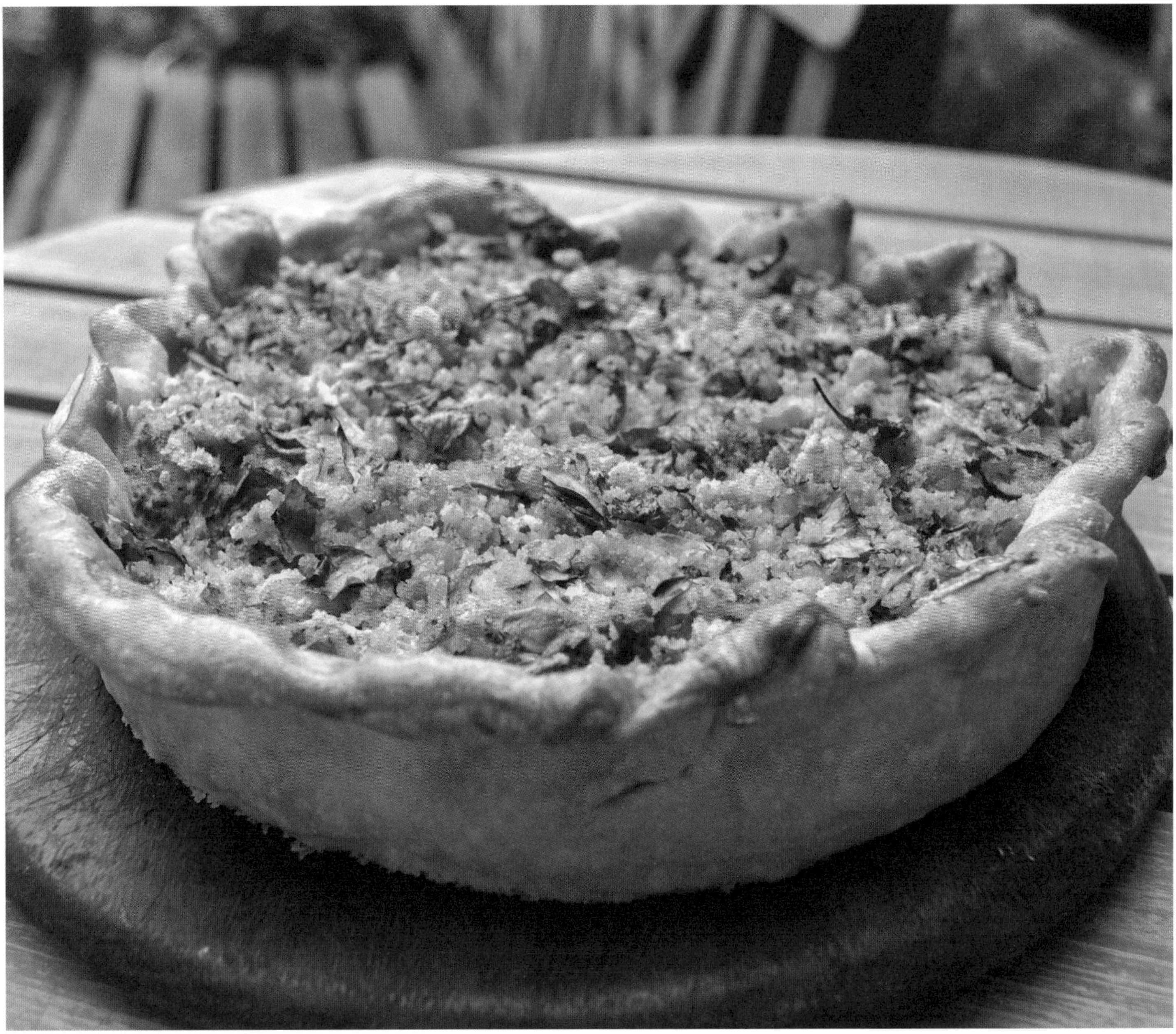

Salmon Pye.

Henry Howard. 1703. 'England's Newest Way in Cookery.'

Make Puff-paste and lay in the bottom of your Patty-pan; then take the middle Pieces of Salmon, Season it high with Salt, Pepper, Cloves and Mace, cut it into three Pieces; then lay a Layer of Butter and a Layer of Salmon till it is laid all out; then make forced Meat of an Eel, and chop it fine with the Yolks of hard Eggs, with two or three Anchovies, Marrow and sweet Herbs, a little grated Bread, a few Oysters, if you have them; lay them round your Pye, and on the Top; season them with Salt and Pepper, and other Spices as you please.

Ingredients

450-500g salmon fillet, with the skin removed and cut into chunks

2-3 teaspoons of ground mace

A pinch of ground cloves

Salt and pepper

Puff pastry

30g butter

Forcemeat:

75g breadcrumbs

3 anchovies and 3 teaspoons of the oil from the jar or tin

50g courgette, grated (to replace the marrow)

20g herbs such as parsley, dill or coriander, leaves chopped

2 hard boiled egg yolks, chopped

Method

1. To make the forcemeat, mix the breadcrumbs with the chopped anchovies and oil from the jar, the courgette, herbs and egg yolks, and season well.

2. Cut the salmon into thin slices then season with mace, cloves, salt and pepper.

3. Roll out the pastry and use to line a deep cake tin with a removable base, or 4-6 individual tart tins.

4. Place the salmon in the pastry case, then spread the forcemeat over this and dot with the butter. Bake for about 20 minutes, oven 180°c, gas 4.

Note: I have omitted the eel, which was plentiful at the time but which is now scarce, as well as unpopular in this country. I also left out the oysters, which are now too expensive for everyday use. I tried tinned oysters, but the taste was overpowering.

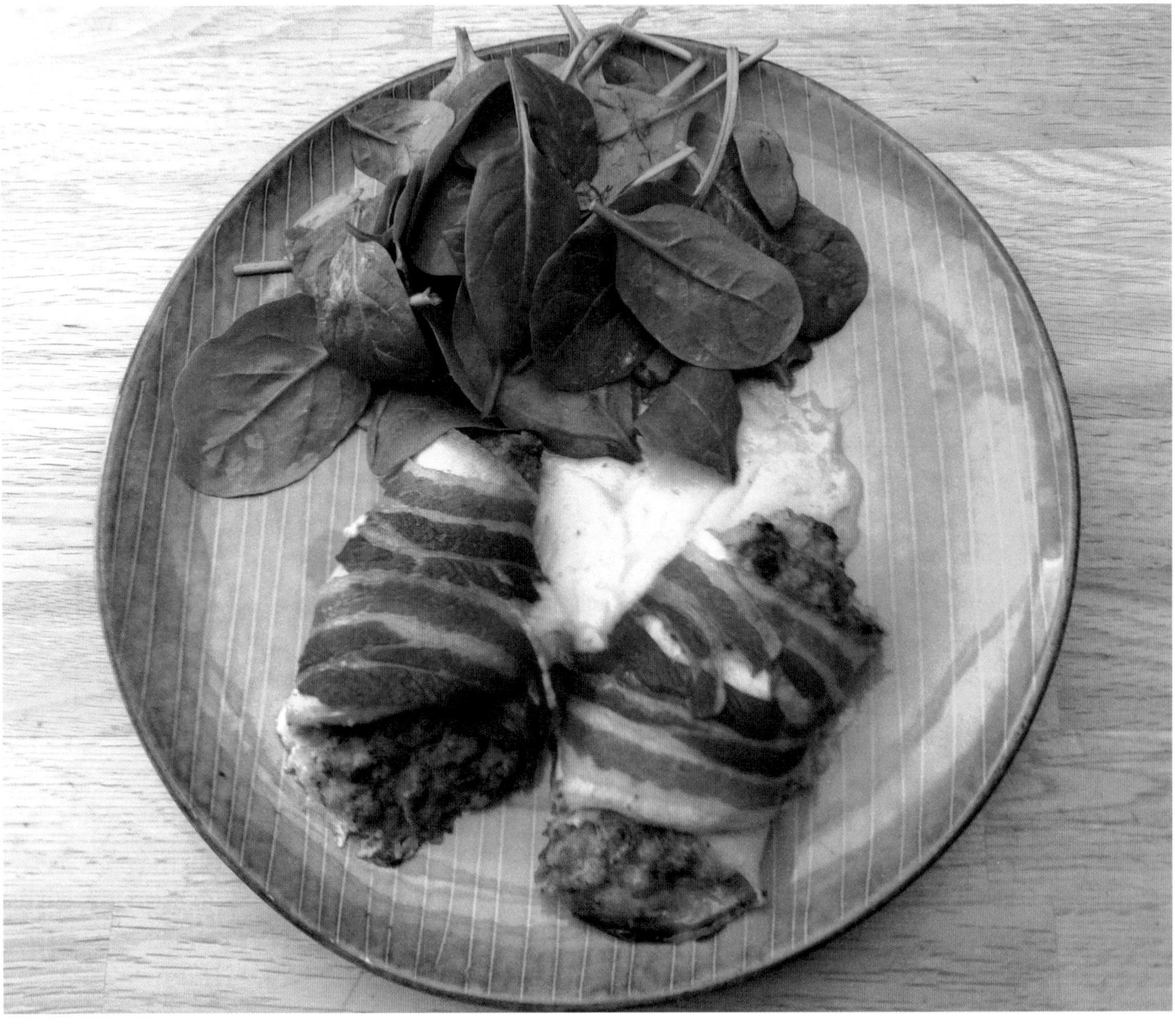

Fillet of Sole à l'Italienne.

Ingredients

4 sole fillets, trimmed (use these trimmings to make stock, by cooking them in water with a carrot, a stick of celery, a little onion and herb. Strain into a jug)

1 egg yolk

8 rashers of streaky bacon

For the stuffing (or 'farce'):

1 sole fillet, skin removed - optional

50g streaky bacon roughly chopped

1 shallot, roughly chopped

2 anchovies

2-4 tablespoons of parsley, chopped

30g breadcrumbs soaked in 30ml cream

1 egg white, whipped lightly

Salt and pepper

For the sauce: (an Italian white sauce is made with rich stock, and some cream)

25g butter

25g flour

150ml fish stock (made as above) – or chicken stock if you prefer

50ml cream

2 tablespoons of grated Parmesan (optional)

Frederick Nutt. 1809. 'The Imperial and Royal Cookbook.'

Fillet a pair of soles; scrape two of the fillets, and as much fat bacon; put it into the mortar, with a little parsley and shalots, all chopped very fine; rub it about the mortar a few minutes; put in half the crumb of a French roll that has been soaked in cream; mix them together; then beat up the white of an egg, and put it in the mortar, with a little pepper and salt, and two anchovies, washed, boned, and chopped very fine; take it all out of the mortar; flat the fillets of soles, brush them over with egg, then spread the farce on, and roll them up; put them into a tart pan, (first covering the bottom with bacon); add a few spoonfuls of stock; cover the fillets with bacon; put them in a slow oven for half an hour, then dish them, and pour white Italian sauce over them.

Method

1. To make the stuffing, blend the sole (if using), bacon, shallot, anchovies and parsley. Mix in the breadcrumbs and cream and the egg white, then season.

2. Brush each sole fillet with some egg yolk then season lightly.

3. Divide the stuffing between the sole fillets then roll them up and wrap each in two rashers of bacon (stretch each rasher to make it go further; the filling will overflow, but just push it back in). Place them in a buttered ovenproof dish, spaced out so that they don't touch. This allows the bacon to become crisp (this is why I have omitted the stock at this stage, as this makes it soggy).

4. Bake at 180°c, gas 4, for 45-50 minutes, until the bacon is golden.

5. To make the sauce, melt the butter in a saucepan then add the flour. Cook gently, stirring, for a few minutes then gradually add the stock. Stir the sauce as it thickens then add the cream and seasoning, and Parmesan if you like.

6. When the sole has cooked, pour the sauce over and serve.

Note: you can use plaice fillets instead of sole, to make the dish less expensive.

The forcemeat can be made without the sole, to reduce the cost of the dish.

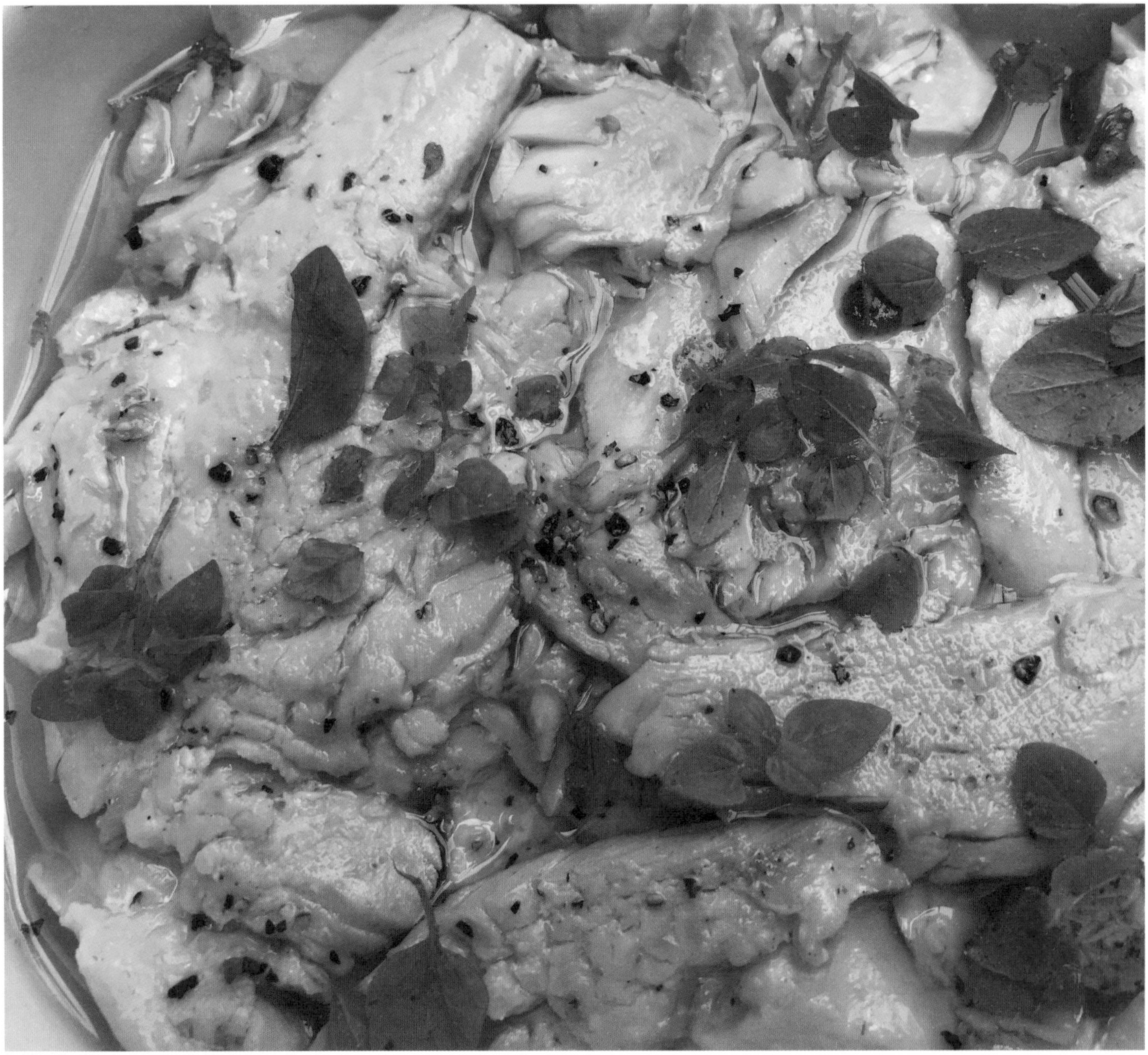

To Marinate Trout.

Francis Collingwood and John Woollams. 1792. 'The Universal Cook.'

Fry your trout in oil sufficient to cover them, and put them in when the oil is boiling hot. When they are crisp, lay them to drain till they are cold, and then take some white wine and vinegar, of each an equal quantity, with some salt, whole pepper, nutmeg, cloves, mace, sliced ginger, savory, sweet marjoram, thyme, rosemary, and two onions. Let these boil together a quarter of an hour. Then put the fish into a stewpan, pour the marinade hot to them, and put in as much oil as white wine and vinegar, which must be according to the quantity of your fish, as the liquor must cover them. Serve them up with oil and vinegar.

Ingredients

4 trout fillets – about 700g - trimmed

100ml oil

Salt and pepper

100ml white wine

100ml cider or white wine vinegar

1 onion, chopped

1 teaspoon of ground nutmeg

A pinch of ground cloves

1 teaspoon of ground mace

2 teaspoons of grated ginger

1-2 sprigs marjoram

1-2 sprigs thyme

1-2 sprigs rosemary

Method

1. Heat the oil in a frying pan then fry the trout fillets over a high flame, turning once.

2. Place the trout in a serving dish and remove the skin and any bones. Sprinkle with some flaked sea salt and freshly ground black pepper.

3. Pour the wine and vinegar into the pan then add the onion, spices and herbs. Season.

4. Simmer over a low heat for 15 minutes then pass through a sieve and pour over the trout fillets. Allow to cool.

Soups, Suppers and Snacks

'Four rows of illuminated lamps round the Rotunda, in many varying forms, as baskets of flow-ers, wreaths of roses. All the boxes were form'd like Turkish tents, with each a festoon curtain that drew up at once when the suppers were placed in the inside, which was done by a gallery being made round the Rotunda behind. This must have had a wonderful pretty effect, as each box was well illuminated, a waiter at each in a Spanish dress, and a gentleman out of livery.' (Ranelagh)

Caroline Powys.
'Diaries of Mrs. Philip Lybbe Powys of Hardwick House. 1756-1808'.

Early in the 18th century there was no lunch as we know it, but it was common to have something light to eat at some point during the day. This became known as luncheon or 'nuncheon', or *'as much food as one's hand can hold'.* (1755. Dr. Johnson.) As time went on this meal became more substantial, and Jane Austen described an informal mid-day meal at Pemberley, where they were served *'cold meat, cake, and a variety of all the finest fruits in season.'* (1813. 'Pride and Prejudice')

Snacks were served in the fashionable tea or coffee houses, which were popular as meeting places. Coffee houses had a variety of surprising functions, such as doctors' surgeries or even as covers for brothels. Tobias Smollet described a woman who: *'set up a coffee-house among the hundreds of Drury, where she entertained gentlemen with claret, arrack, and the choice of half a dozen of damsels, who lived in her house.'* (1748. 'Roderick Random.')

Others were more respectable, so women could visit them. In 'Evelina', Frances Burney described a trip to a coffee house: *'When the opera was over, we went into a place called the coffee-room, where ladies as well as gentlemen assemble. There are all sorts of refreshments, and the company walk about, and chat, with the same ease and freedom as in a private room.'* (1778)

Chocolate houses were also fashionable, and the people could meet their friends to enjoy a rich chocolate drink, poured from a special chocolate pot. The most famous was White's Chocolate House in the fashionable St James Street, owned by an Italian named Frances White.

Various versions of fast food were available, such as Mr. Gill's shop in Bath, where one could buy: *'a jelly, a tart, or a small bason of vermicelli.'* (1771. Tobias Smollett. 'Humphrey Clinker.')

If you wanted to sit down to eat, inexpensive food was served in 'dives', or 'chop houses', known for their fast service and traditional English food. A famous example in London was Dolly's in Queen's Head Passage, where dishes were: *'served as fast as they are cooked'.* (1771. Tobias Smollett. 'Humphrey Clinker.')

People could also eat a fixed-price meal in an 'ordinary'. Tobias Smollett described one in a cellar, where they were *'almost suffocated with the steams of boiled beef, and surrounded by a company of hackney-coachmen, chairmen, draymen, and a few footmen ... who sat eating shin of beef, tripe, cow-heel or sausages ...our reckoning amounting to two pence halfpenny each, bread and small beer included.'* (1748. 'Roderick Random.')

In the summer, picnicking was popular and in 'Sense and Sensibility', Sir John Middleton provided *'cold ham and chicken out of doors'*. (1811. Jane Austen.) In 'Emma', a picnic was arranged by Mrs. Elton and Mr. Weston, which included pigeon-pies and other showy dishes, despised by Emma who had wanted to organise the picnic in a *'quiet, unpretending, elegant way, infinitely superior to the bustle and preparation ... and picnic parade of the Eltons and the Sucklings.'* (1815. Jane Austen.)

Wealthy families liked to remain within their grounds, or those of their friends, and consumed their picnics in buildings such as temples or rotundas. In her diary, Caroline Powys described a meal 'in a little temple' where they were given an *'elegant collation of fruit, cakes, cream, placed in the most neat and rustic manner imaginable.'* (1756-1808)

Outdoor dining reached its pinnacle in the pleasure gardens of London. At Ranelagh there were 52 supper boxes arranged around a huge outdoor fireplace. However, the food was often expensive and at Vauxhall their famous ham was cut so thin that the carver claimed that he could cover the whole of the gardens with the meat from a single ham.

At balls, a supper was provided halfway through the evening. The music stopped and everyone went through to a room where a vast array of food was laid out. This was generally very impressive, and Caroline Powys wrote that Lord Villiers spent £1000 on the supper he provided for his ball in 1777.

Eggs au Miroir.

William Verral. 1759. 'A Complete System of Cookery.'

For this you must have a dish that will bear the fire, rub the bottom with a bit of butter or oil, sprinkle a morsel of green onion and parsley minced, a little pepper, salt and nutmeg, set your dish upon a chaffing-dish of charcoal, break in as many fresh eggs as will almost fill it, pour over them as much cream as your dish will well hold; when it is just boiling dash with a spoon the cream over the tops, that they may be equally done, squeeze in the juice of an orange or lemon, and serve it up.

Ingredients

10g butter at room temperature

2 spring onions, chopped

1 tablespoon of parsley, chopped

Salt and pepper

1 teaspoon of ground nutmeg

6 eggs

100ml double cream

Juice of an orange or a lemon

Method

1. Rub an ovenproof dish with the butter and sprinkle over the spring onions and parsley. Season with salt, pepper and nutmeg.

2. Break the eggs carefully into the dish then pour over 50ml cream.

3. Bake in the oven at 160°c, gas 3, for about 15 minutes until the eggs are set. Squeeze over the orange or lemon juice then spoon over the rest of the cream.

Note: this is good made in six individual ramekin dishes. The name implies that the resulting dish should be as clear or shining as a looking glass.

Macaroni à la Parmesan.

The sons of wealthy families, who went on the 'Grand Tour', always went to Italy. They often developed an appreciation of Italian food during their stay, and when they returned demanded that their cooks learn to make their favourite dishes.

Richard Briggs. 1788. 'The English Art of Cookery.'

Take a quarter of a pound of small pipe macaroni, put it into two quarts of boiling water, with a bit of butter, and boil it till it is tender; then strain it in a sieve and let it drain, grate half a pound of Parmesan cheese, put the macaroni into a stew-pan, with a gill of cream, two ounces of butter, a few bread-crumbs, and half the cheese, stir it about till the cheese and butter are melted; then put the macaroni into a dish, sprinkle the rest of the cheese over it, and with a salamander or hot iron make it of a fine brown, and send it to table as hot as possible.

Ingredients

110g macaroni

60g butter

150ml double cream

200g Parmesan

Freshly ground black pepper

2 tablespoons of fresh breadcrumbs

Method

1. Boil some water and add the macaroni with 10g of the butter and a little salt. Cook until tender – about 10 minutes.

2. Strain the pasta and return to the pan. Add the cream, the rest of the butter and 100g Parmesan. Stir gently until the butter has melted then season with the pepper (you shouldn't need salt as the Parmesan is quite salty). Pour into a buttered ovenproof dish.

3. Mix the rest of the Parmesan with the breadcrumbs and sprinkle over the top of the macaroni.

4. Put it under the grill to brown or into the oven at 180°c, gas 4, for 15 minutes.

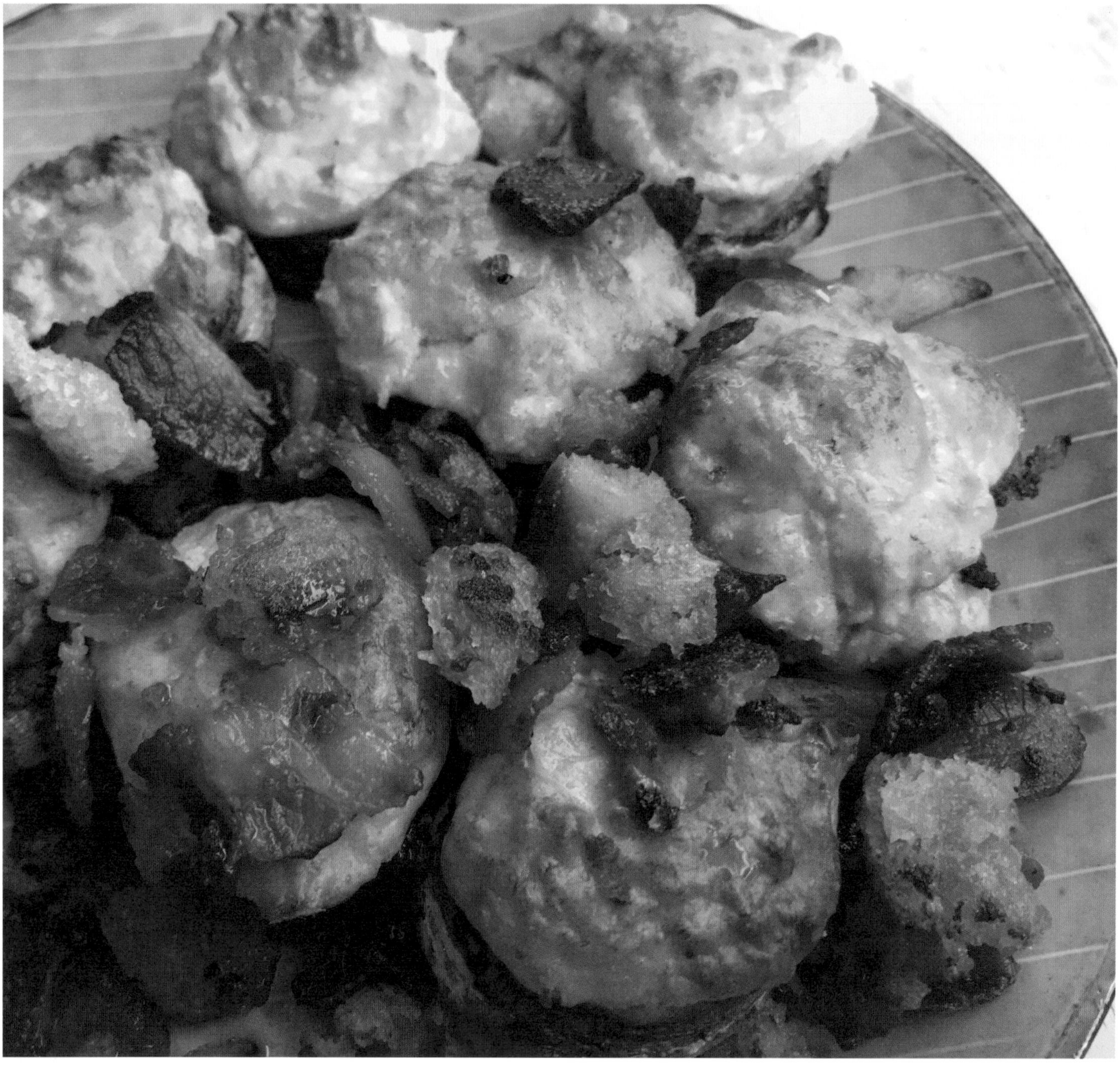

To farce Mushrooms.

The cookery writer John Farley believed that mushrooms could cause *'heart-burns, sicknesses, vomitings, diarrhoeas, dysenteries, and other dangerous symptom.'* (1792. 'The Universal Cook.')

Francis Collingwood and John Woollams disagreed, and in their chapter on the management of the kitchen garden, they described the process for getting mushroom 'spawn' from: *'places where horse dung and litter has been of any long continuance, and moderately dry.'* (1792. 'The Universal Cook.')

John Nott. 1723. 'The Cook and Confectioner's Dictionary.'

Make a Farce with Veal, or the Breast of Pullet, Bacon, Beef-marrow, and the crumb of a French Roll soak'd in Cream, and the Yolks of a couple of Eggs, season'd with Salt, Pepper; and Nutmeg. Let the Mushrooms be well pick'd, and the Stalks pull'd off; then farce them with this Farce, and put them into a Tart-pan, then set them into an oven, and bake them; when they are done, dish them, pour to them some Beef-Gravy, and serve them up.

Ingredients

15g butter

4 large mushrooms, or 8 medium mushrooms, stalks removed

Salt and pepper

50g chicken breast (uncooked)

50g breadcrumbs soaked in 100ml cream

50g bacon

2 egg yolks

Some grated nutmeg

4 slices of streaky bacon, roughly chopped

1 slice of bread, crusts removed and cubed

Method

1. Generously grease an ovenproof dish with some of the butter.

2. Put the mushrooms in the dish and season them with salt and pepper, then dot them with the rest of the butter.

3. Blend the chicken breast with the breadcrumbs and cream, bacon, egg yolks, salt, pepper and nutmeg.

4. Divide this stuffing (or farce) between the mushrooms.

5. Bake in the oven at 180°c, gas 4, for 30-40 minutes. The mushrooms should be soft and the topping should have browned a little.

6. Fry the streaky bacon and cubed bread together until golden and crisp. Use this as a garnish.

Note: Nott's recipe for gravy is very time-consuming and uses a great deal of meat. It's not really necessary to make gravy, as the dish produces its own juices.

Pease Pottage.

'Pottage' comes from the French word for a pot, and refers to a one-pot dish, semi-liquid and full of nourishing ingredients.

Henry Howard. 1703. 'England's Newest Way in Cookery.'

Take eight Pints of Pease, and six quarts of Water; set them on the Fire together with a large Onion, season them high; let them boil; and when they are enough, strain them through a Cullender, and set them on the Fire again; and when they are boiled, put in four handfuls of Spinage, two Leeks, a little Mint, two spoonfuls of Flour tempered with Water; then put in your Forc'd-meat-balls, and a little after a pound of sweet Butter, keep it stirring till the Butter is melted, then dish it to the Table; don't cut the Herbs small but gross; take care they don't lose their Colour, serve it.

Ingredients

(I have used one eighth of the quantities in the original recipe)

50g butter

1 onion, chopped finely

Half a leek, chopped finely

2 rounded teaspoons of flour

900ml stock

100g spinach, chopped fairly small

2 tablespoons of fresh mint leaves, torn up a little

600g peas, cooked

Salt and pepper

Forcemeat balls (see Henry Howard's recipe on following page)

Method

1. Melt the butter in a large pan and fry the onion and leek until softened (I prefer to fry the vegetables first so that they caramelise, which improves the flavour). Add the flour and cook gently, then pour in the stock and stir to thicken. Simmer for 5 minutes.

2. Add the spinach, mint and peas and season. Stir for a few minutes, until the leaves are just cooked. Take care not to over-cook as it will lose its colour and texture.

3. Pour into bowls to serve, with forcemeat balls on top (if you like).

Forcemeat Balls.

Ingredients

100g pork fillet, chopped

1 tablespoon of chives, chopped

1 tablespoon of the leaves
of herbs such as parsley or
coriander, chopped

50g spinach, chopped

Salt and pepper

1 teaspoon of ground mace

4 anchovies

20g flour

1 egg yolk

20g butter

Henry Howard. 1703. 'England's Newest Way in Cookery.'

Take rabbet, veal or pork; shred it very fine, with a few chives, sweet herbs, and a little spinage to make them look green, season them with salt, pepper, mace, anchovies, marrow or beef suet; cut all these very fine together, and bind them with a little flour, and the yolk of an egg, and rowl up some long, some round; fry them brown and crisp, or stew them as you please.

Method

1. Blend all of the ingredients, apart from the butter, in a food processor.

2. Roll the mixture into smallish balls.

3. Melt the butter in a frying pan and cook the forcemeat balls until golden.

Note: I have left out the beef suet to make the dish lighter.

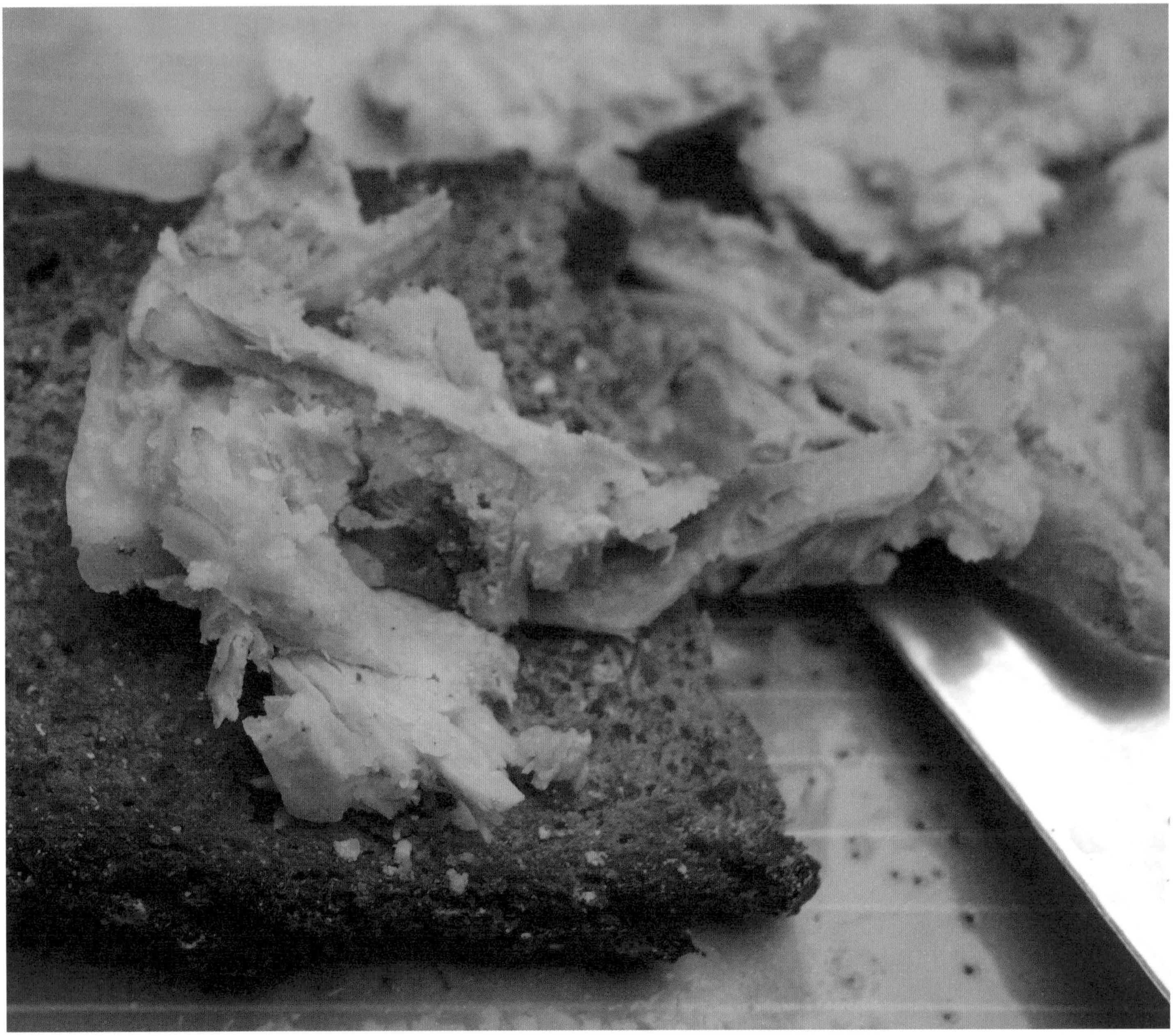

Pheasants, Potted.

Shooting and hunting were popular pursuits for the wealthy, and at Croome Park in Worcestershire, a 'Panorama Tower' allowed a good view of the shoot as well as of the beautiful grounds, designed by Capability Brown.

There were plenty of different types of birds to shoot, with pheasant as the most common, domesticated variety. At Hardwick, the diarist Caroline Powys described a typical sporting event: 'the gentlemen went a shooting, and had great sport, three killed six woodcocks, four rabbits, one hare, but missed a shot at a fine cock-pheasant.' (1899. 'Passages from the Diaries of Mrs. Philip Lybbe Powys of Hardwick House. 1756-1808'.)

Richard Briggs. 1788. 'The English Art of Cookery.'

Pick and draw your game, wipe them clean with a cloth, singe them, season them inside and out well with beaten mace, cloves, nutmeg, pepper, and salt; break the breast bones down as flat as you can, lay them in an earthen pan, cover them with butter, and bake them one hour; when they are taken out of the oven, take them out of the gravy and butter, lay them on a coarse cloth to drain till they are cool, then put them into pots breast upwards, and cover them half an inch thick above the breasts with clarified butter; when they are cold tie white paper over them.

Ingredients

2 pheasant breasts

1 teaspoon of ground mace

Half a teaspoon of ground nutmeg

A pinch of ground cloves

Salt and pepper

75g butter

A couple of bay leaves to decorate

Method

1. Trim any stringy ligaments from the breasts. Season with mace, nutmeg, cloves, salt and pepper.

2. Heat 10g butter in an ovenproof frying pan and fry the pheasant breasts briefly over a high heat until brown on all sides, then turn down the heat and cook for a few more minutes on each side.

3. Allow to cool then cut or tear the meat into strips. Place these in a dish then pour over any juices from the pan. Press the meat down and top with the bay leaves.

4. Heat the rest of the butter gently then leave to cool until it separates. Skim off any scum then pour the top part of this clarified butter over the pheasant, leaving the milky curds behind. Cover and refrigerate.

Note: If you prefer you can use the crown from a whole pheasant. (The carcass can be used to make stock.) I have included the juices from the pan as they contain so much flavour. Pouring the juices in before the clarified butter avoids spoiling the appearance of the dish (I have used less butter to make the dish less fatty). In Smith's recipe for clarified butter, he adds a little orange flower water, which adds an interesting flavour.

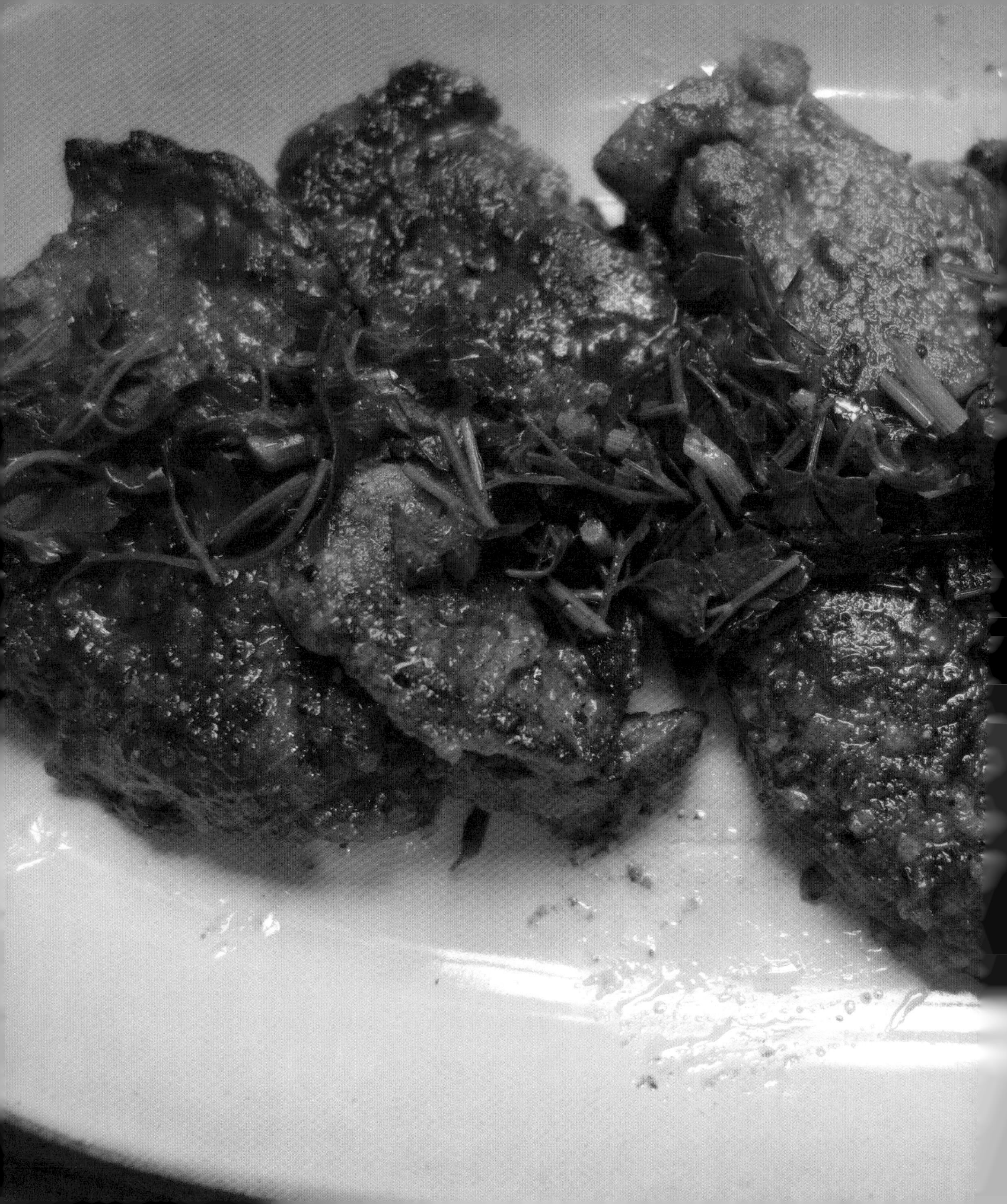

To Marinate Pigeons.

Pigeon meat was very tender as the 'squabs' were eaten young before they had learned to fly. Their dung was used as a fertilizer and to soften leather, as well as to make gunpowder (it contains saltpeter). Their feathers were used in pillows and bedding – softer than the straw that was used in poorer homes.

Compared to chickens, pigeons were easier to manage. They foraged for their own food and were edible in twenty-eight days.

Ingredients

8 spring onions, chopped

Juice of a lemon

2 tablespoons of white wine vinegar or cider vinegar

1 bay leaf

1 teaspoon of allspice

A pinch of ground cloves

Salt and pepper

8 pigeon breasts (this is far simpler to prepare and eat than using whole pigeons)

20g butter

20g flour

4 tablespoons of parsley leaves

2 tablespoons of oil

John Nott. 1723. 'The Cook and Confectioner's Dictionary.'

Make a Marinade of Lemon-juice, Verjuice or Vinegar, Salt, Pepper, Cloves, a Bay Leaf and Chibbols, slit your Pigeons on the Back, or cut them into Quarters, that the Marinade may penetrate into the Flesh, and let them lie in it for two or three Hours; then dip them into Paste, or else flour them, and fry them gently; when they are enough, serve them up to Table hot with fry'd Parsley upon them, and Rape Vinegar, and white Pepper round about them.

Method

1. Gently cook the spring onions in the lemon juice, vinegar, bay leaf, allspice, cloves and seasoning until softened then allow to cool.

2. Cover the pigeon breasts with this mixture and chill for a couple of hours.

3. Scrape the marinade off the pigeon breasts.

4. Heat the butter in a frying pan.

5. Cut the pigeon breasts in half horizontally then coat them in the flour, with a little salt and pepper.

6. Fry them in the butter for a few minutes. Place them on a serving dish and keep them warm.

7. Fry the parsley in the juices in the pan over a high flame for a minute then scatter this over the pigeon breasts

Note: chibbols are green onions or young leeks.

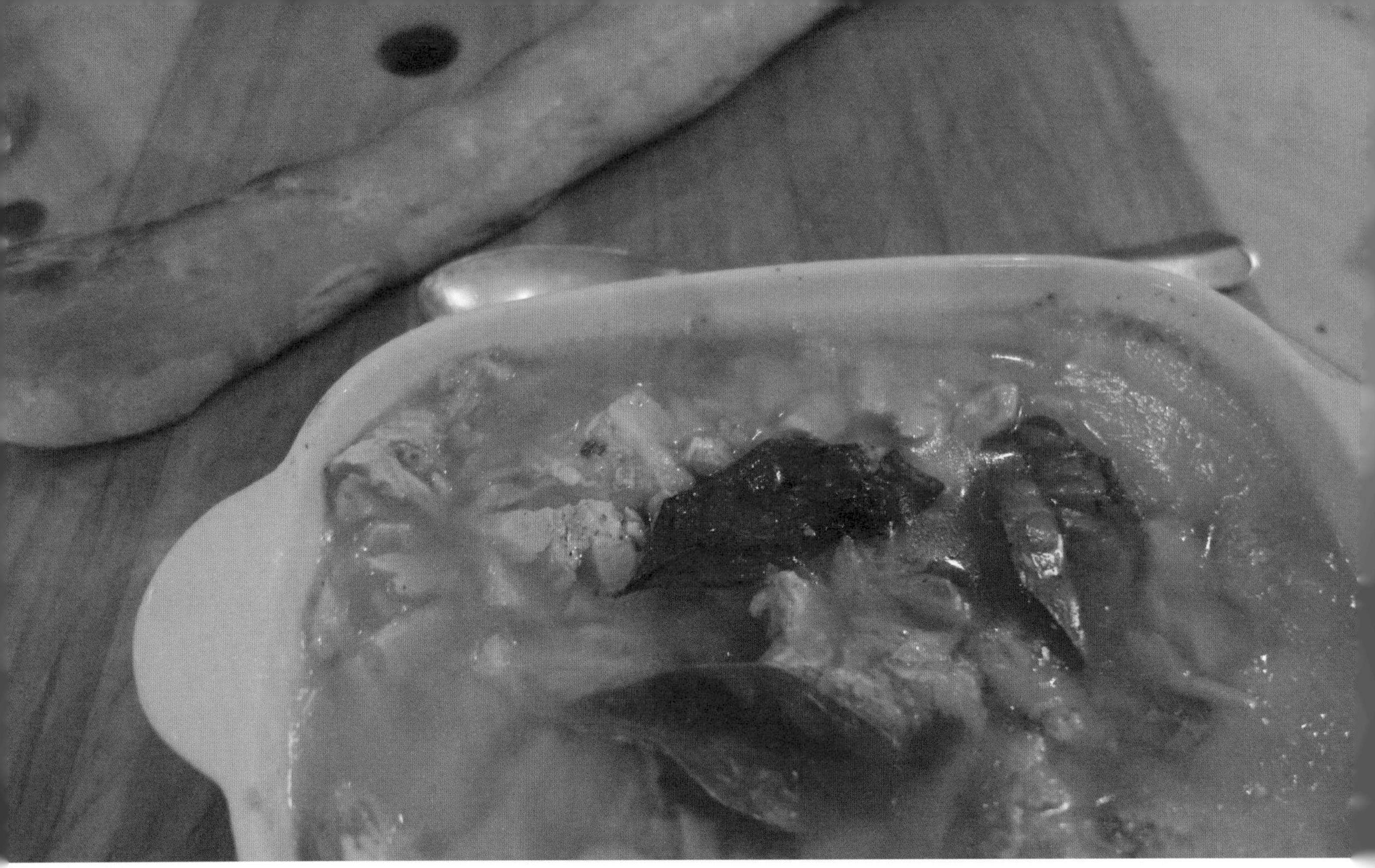

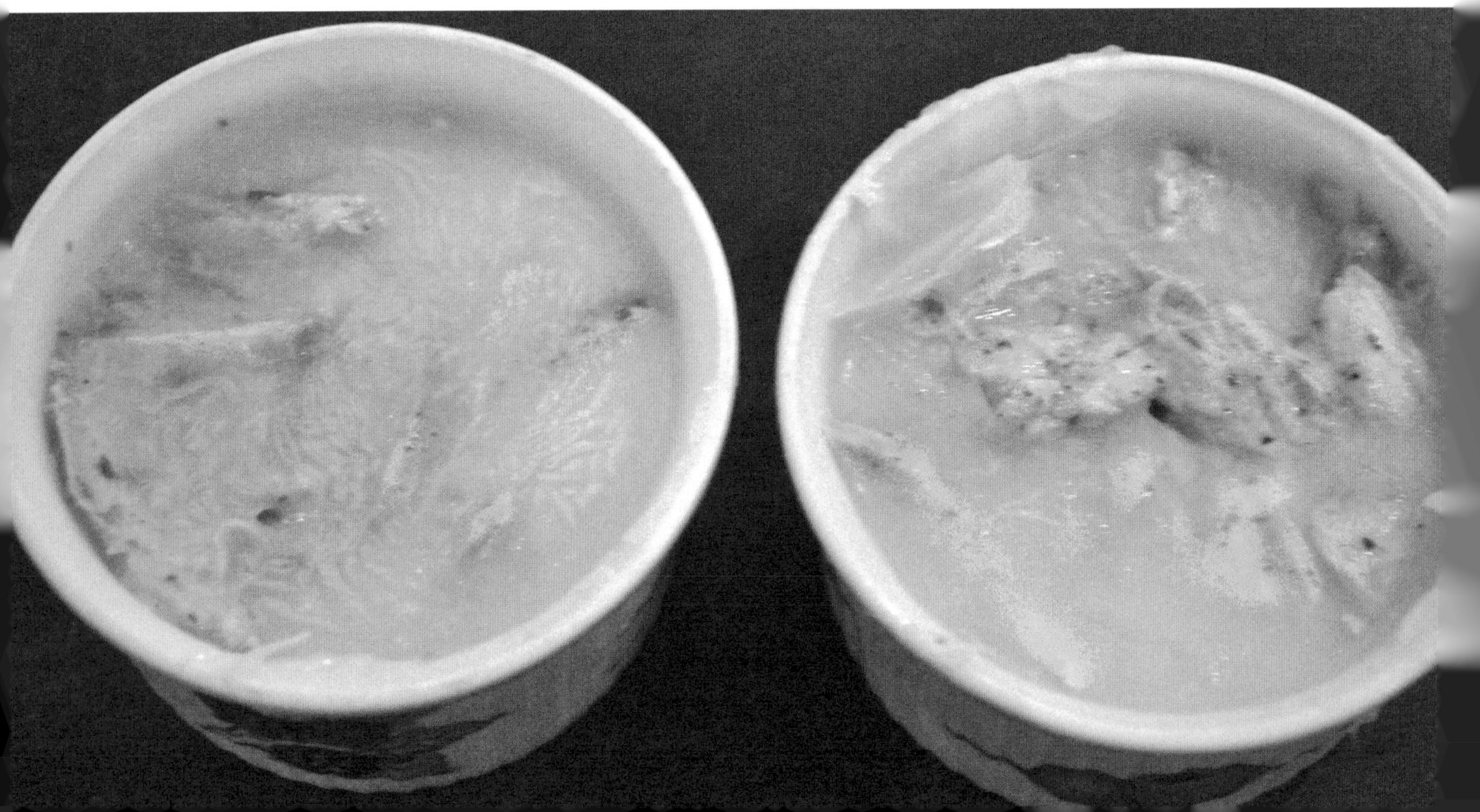

Potted Salmon.

Henry Howard. 1717. 'England's Newest Way.'

'The earliest (salmon) that comes in season to the London market is brought from the Severn, and begins to come into season the beginning of November, but very few so early, perhaps not above one in fifty, as many of them will not shoot their spawn till January, or after, and then continue in season till October, when they begin to get very thin and poor.' (The Cook's Oracle and Housekeeper's Manual. 1817)

In the workhouse at St. Martin's in the Fields, records show that the inmates were allowed salmon *'once in the season'.* (The State of the Poor; Volume 2 by Sir Eden, 1797). Few of the other workhouses provided any fish at all.

Take what piece you have, season it with Cloves, Mace, a little Salt and Pepper, two Bay-leaves: Put it into a Pot with as much melted Butter as will cover it; then set it in the Oven with Manchet-bread, and when it's baked take it out of the Pot, and put it into the Pot you intend to keep it in, and pour the Butter, and clarifie it, and cover it very well; and if you find it's not seasoned high enough, season it higher; then put it into the other Pot; and the same way pot Trout or Eels, only you must bone them.

Ingredients

250g butter, melted

350g salmon fillet

1 teaspoon of ground mace

Half a nutmeg, grated finely

1 teaspoon of sea salt

Freshly ground black pepper

2 bay leaves

Method

1. Pour a little of the butter into an ovenproof dish then add the salmon. Rub the mace, nutmeg, salt and pepper over the salmon. Pour over the rest of the butter and add one bay leaf.

2. Cover and bake in the oven at 180°c, gas 4, for 30 minutes. Take the salmon out of the butter, remove the skin, then break it up and place it in a dish, pressing it down to compact it to make an even surface. Place the other bay leaf on top.

3. Spoon the clear butter from the ovenproof dish through a sieve into a small jug. Allow this to settle (this is a simple version of clarified butter)

4. Pour the remaining juices from the dish over the salmon.

5. Once settled, spoon the clear butter from the top of the jug over the salmon, leaving any sediment behind.

6. This should be served cold, but I like it with the butter only half set, spread thickly over bread or toast.

Note: 'manchet' bread was made from the finest kind of wheat. It was made in the form of a round roll, with a cut down the middle so that it could be split in two. This probably took the same amount of time to cook as the salmon, and they would have been good eaten together.

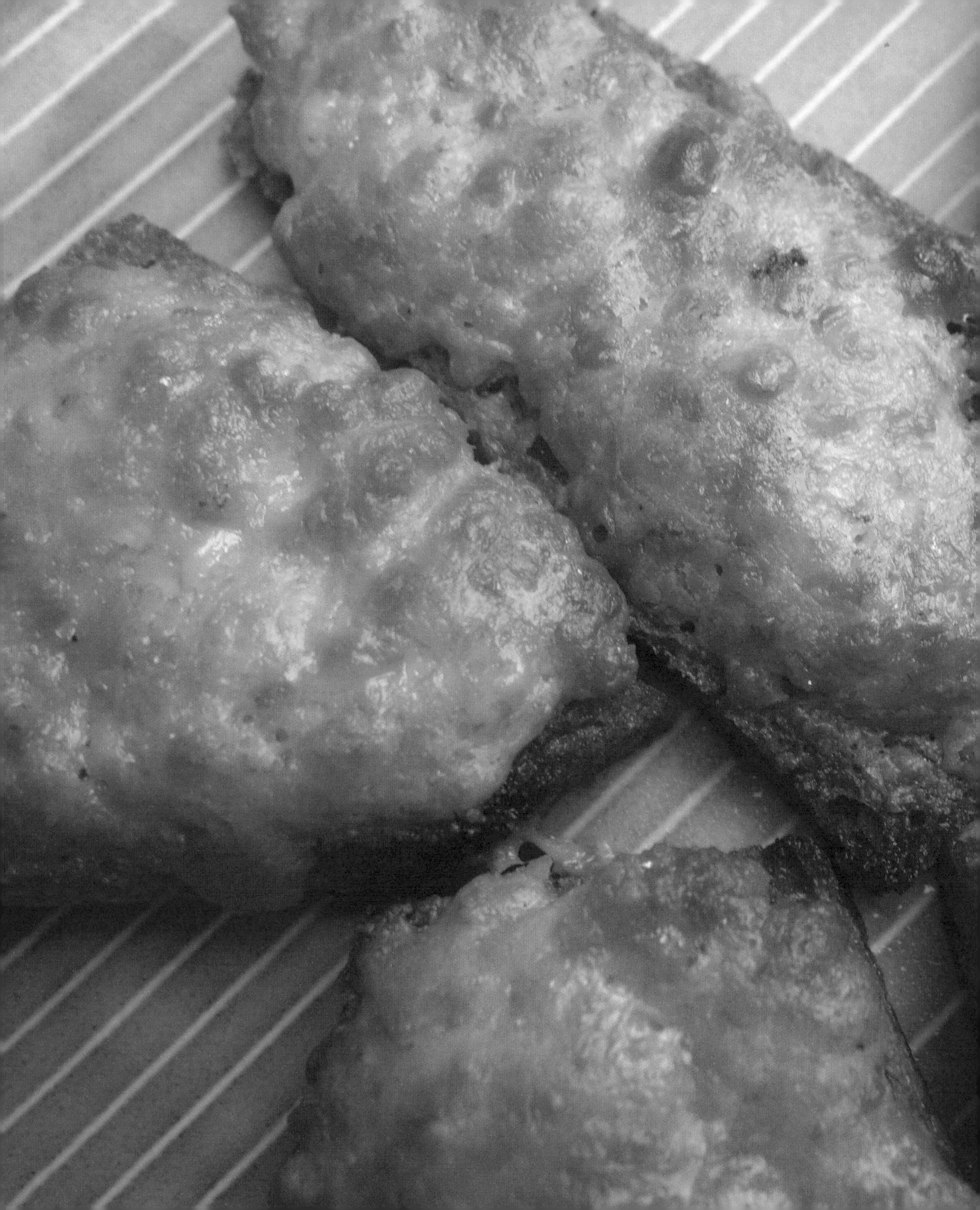

Ramekins.

This is a version of cheese on toast. Other cookery writers like Richard Briggs made it in a similar way, calling them 'Ramaquins on Toasts'. Other methods suggest baking the cheese mixture in a dish in the oven, sometimes with breadcrumbs added to the mix.

The name ramekin was derived from the Flemish 'rammeken', diminutive of 'ram' or cream. Gradually this came to mean cheese, so ramekin dishes are usually cheese dishes.

Robert Smith. 1723. 'Court Cookery'.

Take a Pound of mild Cheese, grate it, and put to it two or three Pats of Butter, and the Yolks of two Eggs; make it up like Paste, spread it on slices of Bread, and bake it in an Oven upon a Pattee-Pan; butter your Pan first.

Ingredients

(I have halved the quantities used in the original recipe)

225g cheese, grated

30g butter at room temperature, and some extra to butter the bread

1 egg yolk

About 6 slices of bread

Method

1. Beat together the cheese, butter and egg yolk until it forms a paste.

2. Butter each slice of bread then cut in quarters and place butter-side down on a baking tray. Spread some of the cheese mixture on each. Bake at 180°c for 10-15 minutes, until crisp and golden.

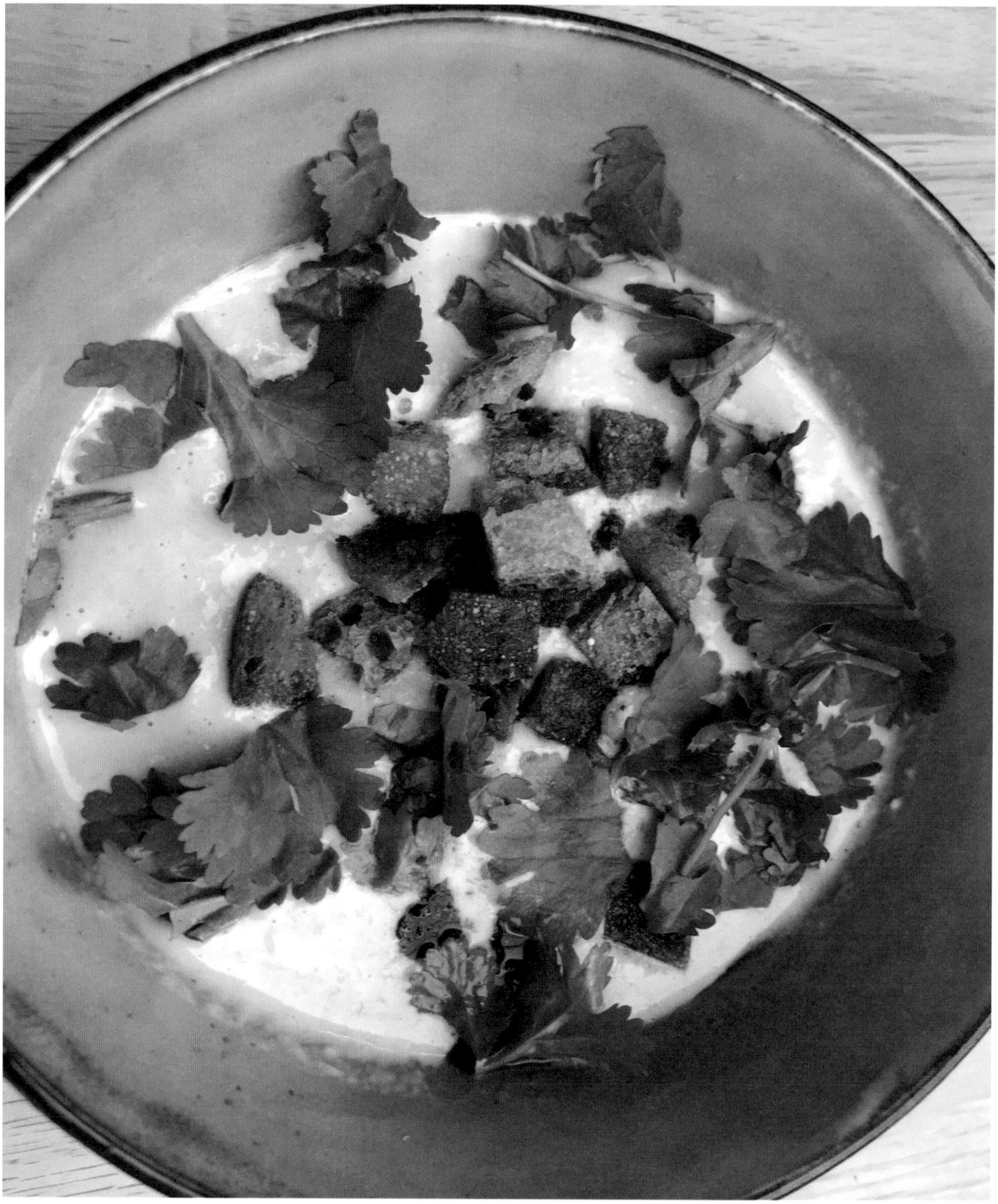

Soup à la Reine.

This is a creamy chicken soup - an early type of white soup. This would have been served as a reviving supper for guests at a ball, which would go on until the early hours of the morning. It could also be served as guests arrived if it was very cold, to warm them up.

Ingredients

(I have greatly reduced the quantities used in the original recipe, and left out the veal as it is not popular these days)

250g gammon

4 chicken thighs

A handful of parsley

1 onion, cut into chunks

1 blade of mace

500ml stock

Salt and pepper

25g almonds, ground

1 roll to make 50g of breadcrumbs (keep the crust)

150ml cream

A little butter

Parsley to garnish

Frederick Nutt. 1809. 'The Imperial and Royal Cookbook.'

Cut a few slices of lean ham, and cover the bottom of a stewpan, that will hold four quarts; cut up two fowls, and put them in a stewpan, with a few slices of veal, some parsley, six onions, a few blades of mace, and about half a pint of water; put it on a slow stove for an hour, to draw down; (take care that it does not catch at the bottom when drawn down, fill up the stewpan with some of your best stock, and let it boil gently for one hour; take out the fowls, and pull the meat from the bones; put it into a mortar, with two ounces of sweet almonds; let it be pounded very fine, so that it will go through a tammy: when beat enough, put it into a small soup-pot that will hold three quarts; put nearly two quarts of stock which the fowls were boiled in, with the crumb of three French rolls; let it boil for one hour, then rub it through a tammy, and add about a pint of good cream that has been boiled; put it in the soup-pot, and put the pot into a stewpan of hot water, and set it by the side of a stove to boil. Before you put it into a tureen, taste it, as perhaps it may want a little salt, or a small bit of sugar: cut the crust of the rolls, which you took the crumb from, into round pieces, about the size of a shilling, and put them into the tureen before the soup is put in.

N.B. All white soups should be warmed by putting the soup-pot into hot water

Method

1. Put the gammon into a pan with the chicken thighs, parsley, onion and mace. Cover with water and simmer gently for an hour, making sure the meat does not stick to the bottom of the pan.

2. Add the stock and some salt and pepper and simmer gently for another hour.

3. Pass the soup through a sieve into a large jug.

4. Remove the chicken meat from the bones.

5. Remove the fat from the gammon.

6. Blend the chicken and gammon with the almonds, breadcrumbs, cream and about 600ml liquid. Pour into a clean pan and warm through then check the seasoning.

7. Chop the crust of the roll into pieces then fry in a little butter until crisp and golden. Scatter these over the soup with a little parsley.

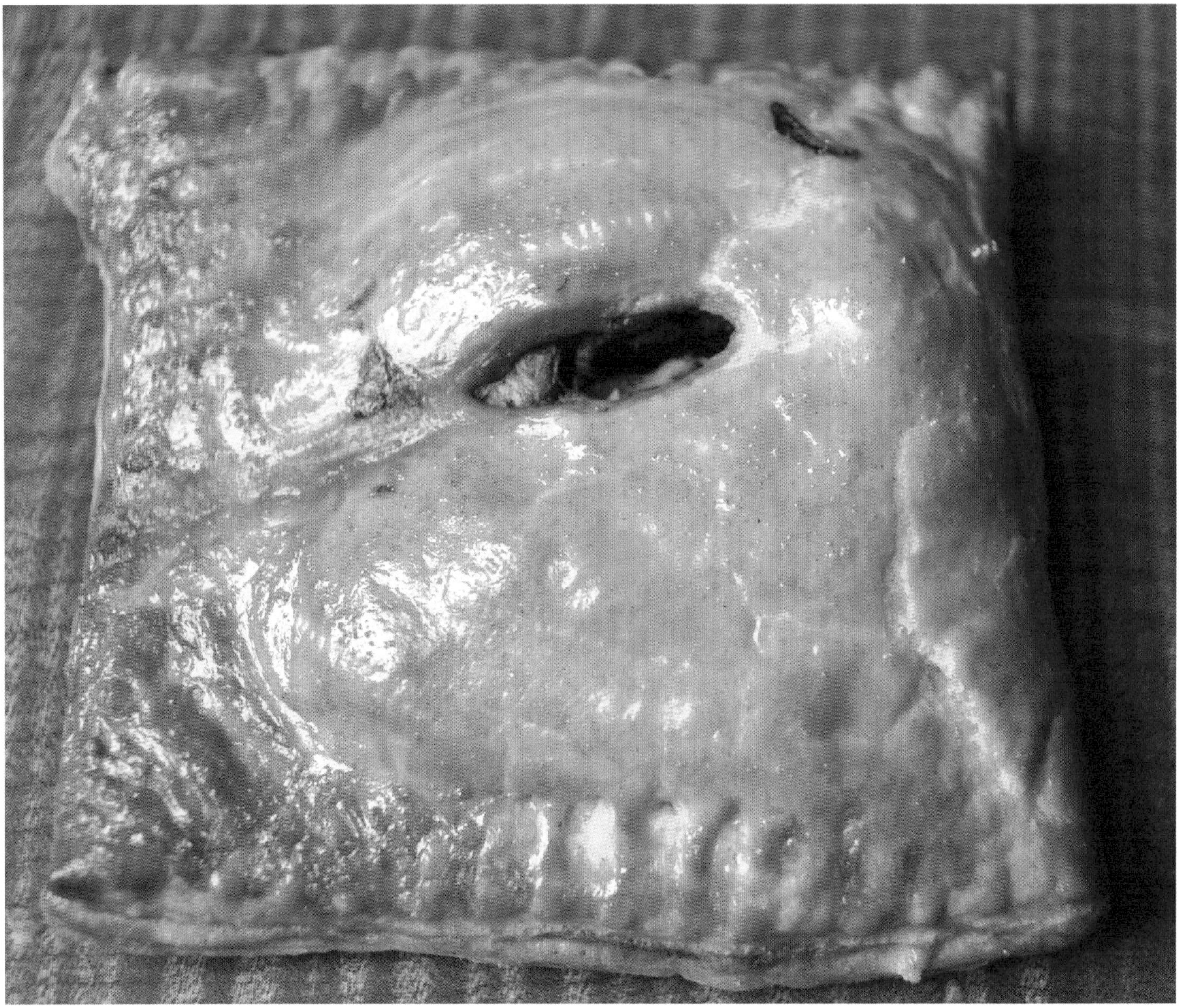

Spinach Tart.

Henry Howard. 1703. 'England 's Newest Way in Cookery.'

Take marrow, spinage, hard eggs, of each a handful, cloves, mace, nutmeg, limon-peel shred very fine; then put in as many currans as you think fit, with raisins stoned, and shred, candied orange and citron peel; sweeten it to your taste; make puff-paste, and make them into little square pasties; bake or fry them.

Ingredients

100g marrow or courgette, chopped finely or grated

100g spinach

Grated zest of an orange and a lemon

20g currants or sultanas

20g candied orange peel or 2 teaspoons sugar

1 hard boiled egg, chopped

Half a teaspoon of ground mace

Half a teaspoon of ground nutmeg

A pinch of ground cloves

1 teaspoon of salt

Puff pastry

A little beaten egg

Method

1. Mix the marrow or courgette, spinach, orange and lemon zest, currants or sultanas, candied orange peel, egg, mace, nutmeg, cloves and salt. Squeeze the mixture together, draining off any excess fluid.

2. Roll out the puff pastry and cut into four rectangles about 10cm x 15cm.

3. Brush the edges of each rectangle with beaten egg then put some of the spinach mixture at one end of each. Fold the pastry over the mixture, press down the edges, make a slit in the top of each, and brush them with beaten egg.

4. Place these on a baking tray dusted with flour then bake them in the oven at 200°c, gas 6, for 15-20 minutes.

Note: this quantity makes 4-6 individual pies. This type of sweet taste in a savoury dish is very typical of Georgian dishes, but may not appeal to everyone. I love it as it takes you by surprise!

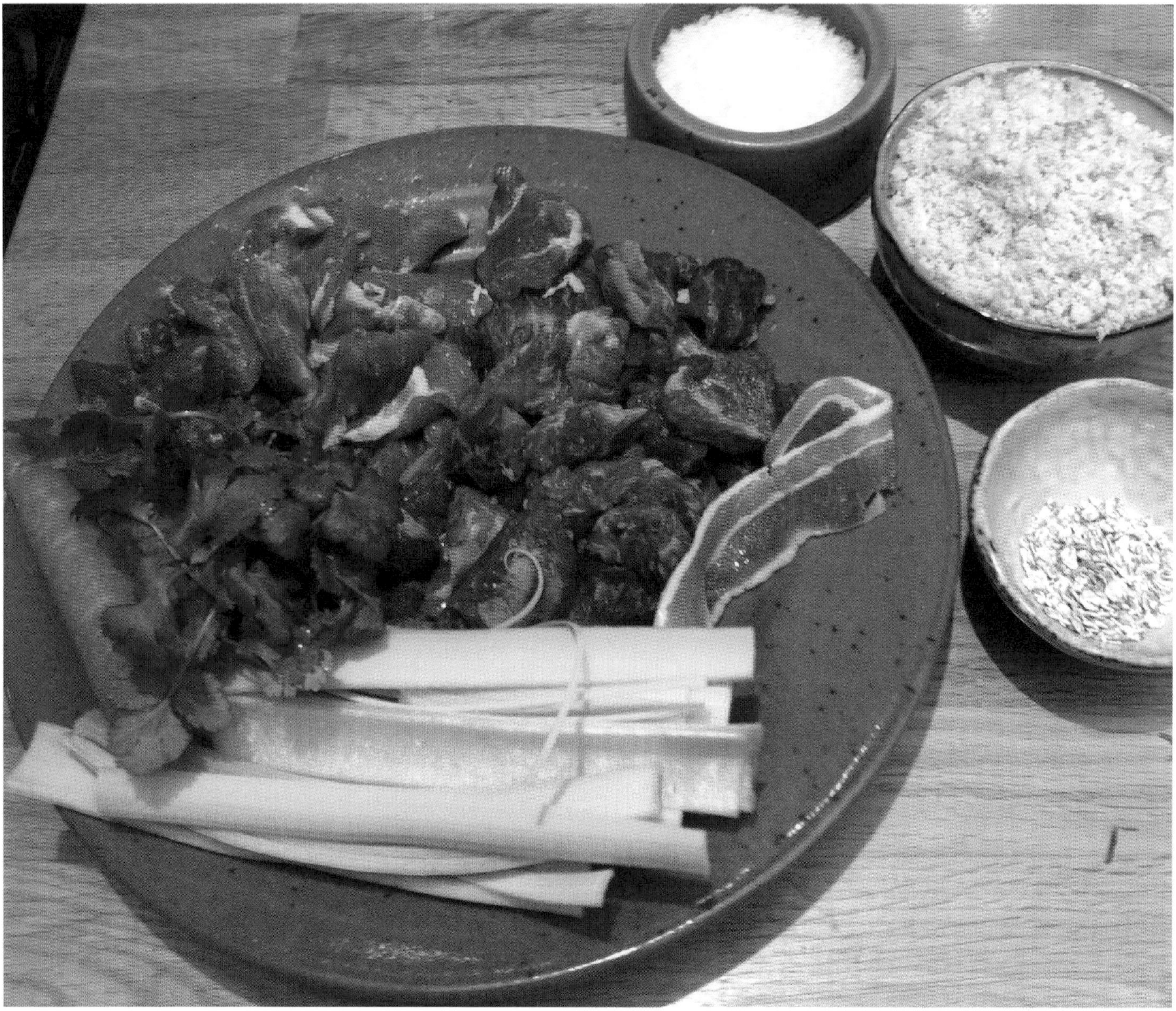

White Soop.

Despite its name, it really doesn't look very white at all. The soup a la reine (earlier in this section) is a whiter soup; other recipes used veal or rice. White soup was not only expensive but involved a laborious process. Mr. Bingley was referring to this when planning the ball at Netherfield. He says: *'as soon as Nicholls has made white soup enough I shall send round my cards.'* (1813. Jane Austen. 'Pride and Prejudice.')

Ingredients

(I have divided the quantities in the original recipe by eight, approximately)

225g beef

170g lamb

1 litre water or stock

1 teaspoon of oatmeal or oats

Half a teaspoon of ground white pepper

1 teaspoon of salt

1 rasher streaky bacon, chopped

1 carrot, finely chopped

½ leek, finely chopped

½ turnip, or white beet, finely chopped, if you can get them (and if you like them)

100g white breadcrumbs

20g leaves of herbs such as sorrel, parsley or coriander, chopped

1 egg yolk

20g butter

Henry Howard. 1703. 'England 's Newest Way in Cookery.'

Take four pound of course Beef, three pound of Mutton, set it on the Fire with seven Quarts of Water, let it boil very slow; skum it clean, and let it boil two Hours; then take the Meat up in a Tray, take up a little of the Liquor and beat out all the Goodness of the Meat, and put in the Liquor again; cut off a pound of each Piece to put in the middle of your Dish; then take two spoonfuls of Oat-meal, ten Corns of white Pepper and a little Salt, a quarter of a pound of Bacon, a Carrot, a Turnip cut in Pieces; then put in half your Soop-herbs, which must be Sorrel, a little white Bete, hard Lettice, a Leek, the quantity of two handfuls in all; cut them gross, and put in half at ten a Clock with the Liquor, and about eleven put in the rest, so let it boil till twelve; then take it off and put it into your Soop-Dish, with the pieces of Meat in the Middle; let it stand over the Stove till one a Clock, then cut in half a half-penny Roll at six Slices, and take five Yolks of Eggs and beat them well into the Soop; then garnish with brown Crust grated round the brims of your Dish.

Method

1. Simmer the beef and lamb in the water or stock for 2 hours. Remove the meat and keep it warm.

2. Add the oatmeal or oats, pepper, salt, bacon, carrot, leek and turnip (if using) to the liquid in the pan. Simmer for an hour.

3. Return the meat to the pan and warm it through.

4. Add half the breadcrumbs to the pan with the herbs and the egg yolk, stir well, then cook gently to thicken the soup.

5. Fry the remaining breadcrumbs in the butter.

6. Put the soup into a dish and place a piece of the meat in the middle. Sprinkle over the fried breadcrumbs and serve.

7. Serve the soup with some breadcrumbs sprinkled over the top.

Note: this soup is very filling, and would be a main dish if you kept the meat as a whole piece, as described in the original recipe.

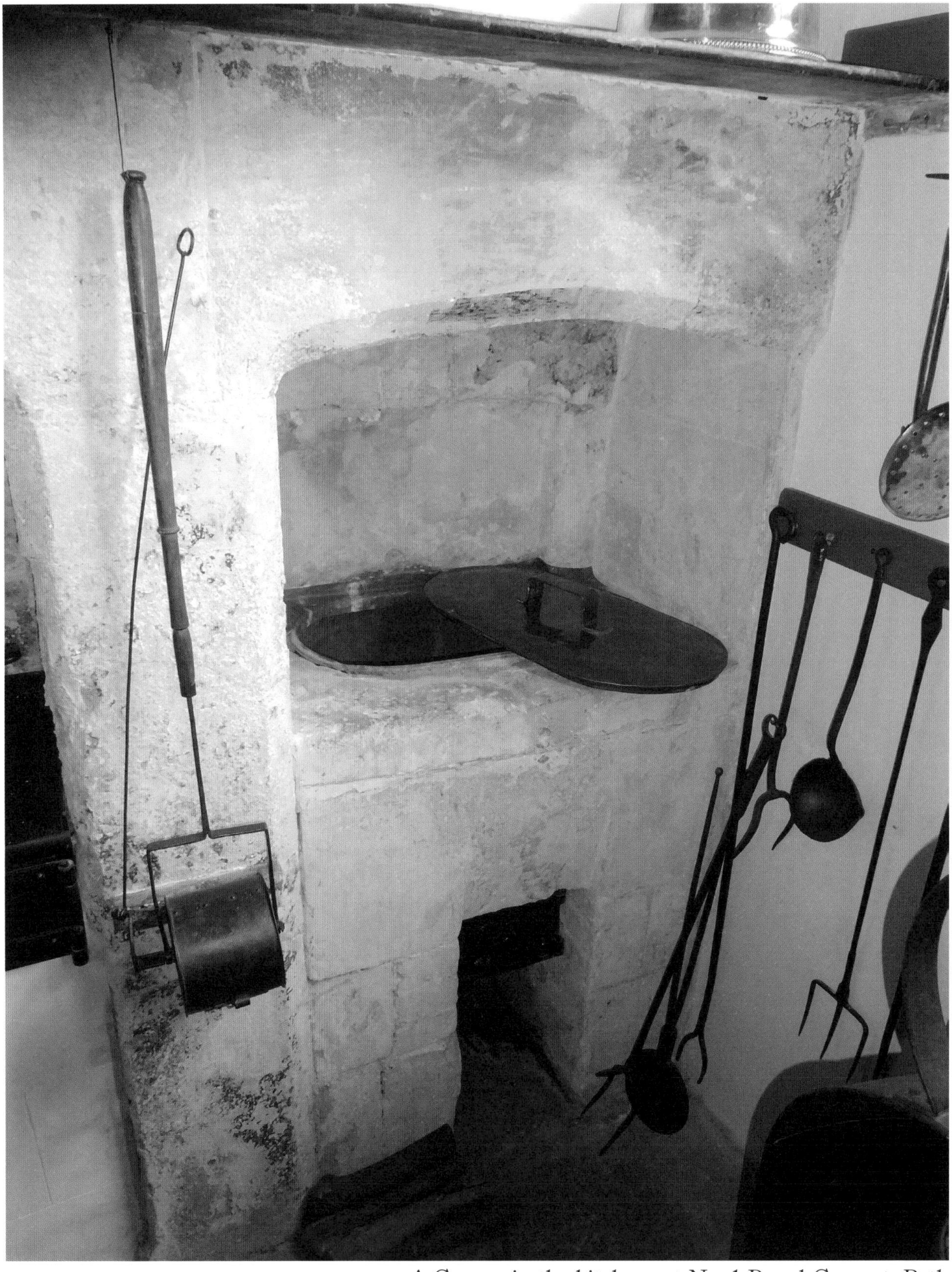

A Copper in the kitchens at No. 1 Royal Crecent, Bath
Reproduced by kind permission of the Bath Preservation Trust

Vegetables

'All kinds of vegetables should have a little crispness; for if you boil them too much, you will deprive them both of their sweetness and beauty.'

John Farley. '1792. The London Art of Cookery.'

Most Georgians considered meat to be the most important element of their diet and it was not easy to convince them to eat vegetables. Tobias Smollet's character, Mr. Lavement, tried in vain to convince his family to share his vegetarian practices, praising *'roots and greens, and decrying the use of flesh, both as a physician and philosopher, but all his rhetoric could not make one proselyte to his opinion, and even the wife of his bosom declared against the proposal.'* (1748. 'Roderick Random.')

George 3rd was unusual in his appreciation of vegetables and simple rustic dishes: *'His Majesty ... feeds chiefly on vegetables, and drinks but little wine.'* (1819. 'Memoirs of Queen Charlotte') Sadly, cartoons of the day mocked his abstemious ways.

A French agronomist named Parmentier recognised the nutritional value of potatoes, which had previously been associated with diseases such as leprosy. He persuaded Marie Antoinette to wear potato flowers to show off their beauty, and her husband, Louis XVI, wore one in his buttonhole. In 1795 the Board of Agriculture produced a pamphlet, 'Hints Respecting the Culture and Use of Potatoes', hoping to encourage farmers to grow them as an energy-rich food that was easy to produce.

Many kitchens had a copper or metal cauldron, used to boil dishes such as pease pudding. In poorer homes, the same cauldron could be used on Mondays to do the washing. I imagine there must often have been a taste of residual soap in dishes produced on Tuesdays. In more affluent homes they would have had more than one copper to avoid this problem.

Oils were imported from Europe, and the cookery writer Charlotte Mason gave advice to those who had not encountered this ingredient in their cooking. *'There are many sorts of oil, but only one used for the table, which is that produced by the olive..... Italian oil is generally the finest. That of Lucca and Florence is particularly esteemed. They make very good oil in France. In the choice of oil, we are to judge by the smell and taste. It should be free from both.'* (1773. 'The Lady's Assistant') Oils were also used in salads and dressings. Jane Austen described Kitty and Lydia Bennet *'dressing a sallad and cucumber'* while they waited for their sisters. (1813. 'Pride and Prejudice.')

Many new plants were imported and brought to physic gardens such as those at Chelsea or Oxford for research. Caroline Powys visited the Oxford Physic Garden in 1759, and described it with enthusiasm in her Journal: *'on each side of the grand entrance is a greenhouse; besides there's a fine hothouse, containing and raising for the garden many thousand plants for the improvement of botanical studies and vegetable philosophy.'* (1899. Diaries of Mrs. Powys of Hardwick House: A.D. 1756-1808'.)

Not everyone liked these additions to the English diet. Samuel Johnson said that a *'cucumber should be well-sliced, dressed with pepper and vinegar, and then thrown out.'* (1791. James Boswell. 'The Life of Samuel Johnson.')

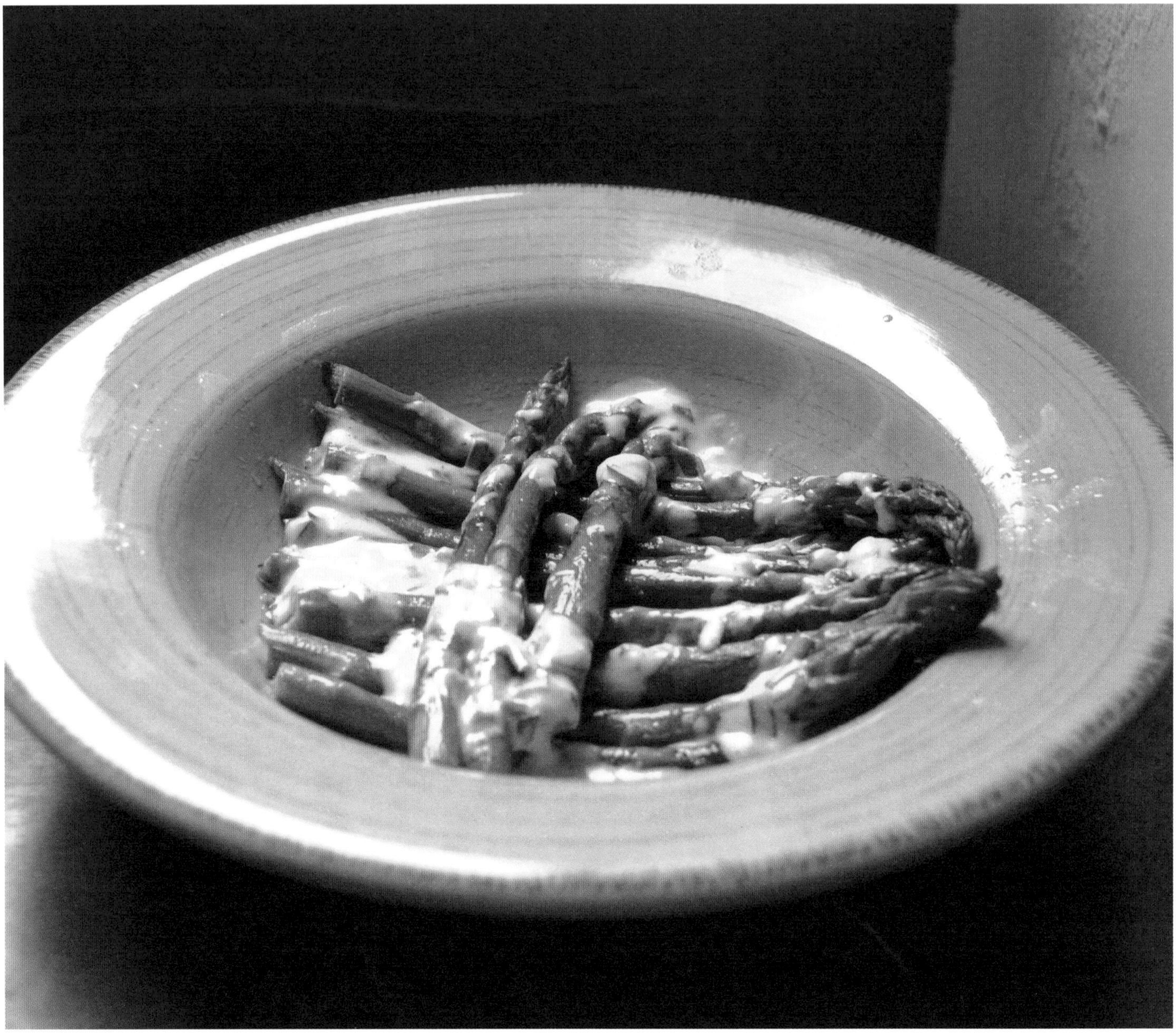

Asparagus in Cream.

Bradley often used herbs and spices in his dishes. The East India Company merchants brought a wide range of spices to London at the time, including mace, nutmeg, cinnamon, turmeric and cayenne. Any of these would work well in this recipe.

Richard Bradley. 1730. 'The Country Housewife.'

Break the Tops of your Asparagus in small Pieces then blanch them a little in boiling Water, or parboil them, after which put them in a Stew-Pan or Frying-Pan with Butter or Hog's-Lard, and let them remain a little while over a brisk Fire, taking care that they are not too greasy, but well drain'd; then put them in a clean Stew-Pan with some Milk and Cream, a gentle Seasoning of Salt and Spice, with a small Bunch of sweet Herbs; and just when they are enough, add to them the Yolks of two or three Eggs beaten, with a little Cream to bind your Sauce.

Ingredients

24 asparagus tips

20g butter

2 teaspoons of turmeric

150ml cream

2 egg yolks

4 tablespoons of the leaves of herbs such as tarragon or chives, chopped

Salt and pepper

Method

1. Blanch the asparagus in salted boiling water for a couple of minutes. Drain.

2. Melt the butter in a frying pan. Add the turmeric and fry gently for a minute or two then add the asparagus.

3. Mix the cream with the egg yolks, herbs and seasoning.

4. Pour this into a clean pan. Heat gently, stirring as the sauce thickens.

5. Add the asparagus, cook for a couple of minutes and serve immediately.

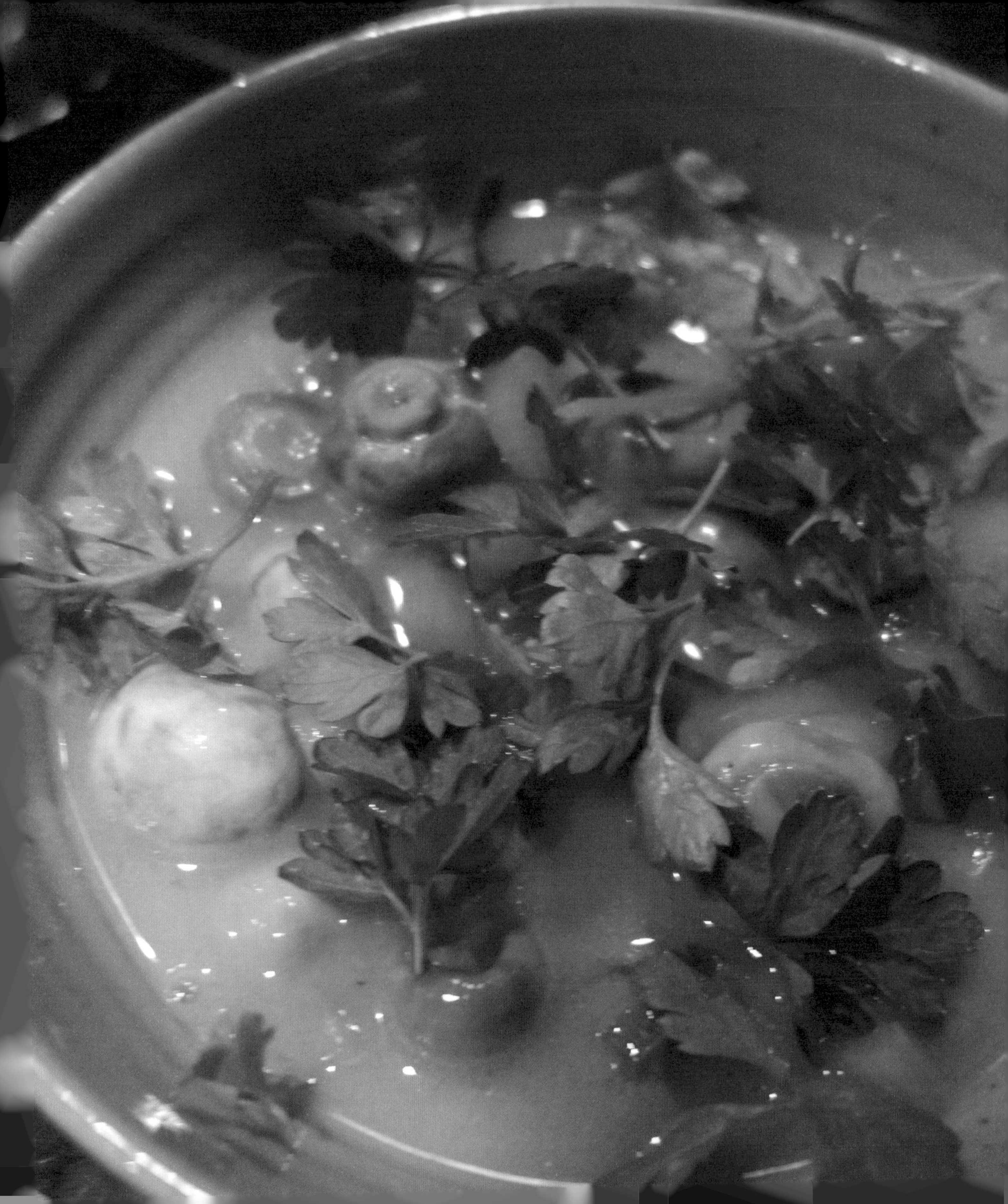

Fricassée of Mushrooms.

William Verral, who ran the White Hart in Lewes, Sussex, had worked as assistant to Clouet, the French cook, learning the basics of French cuisine. This is reflected in many of his recipes, which he passed on to local cooks who wanted to improve their skills.

William Verral, 1759. 'A Complete System of Cookery.'

Clean some nice button mushrooms with flannel and water, wash them in a second, and put them into a stewpan, with a glass of Champagne, Rhenish, or other white wine, a bunch of onions, thyme and parsley, pepper, salt, and a blade of mace, toss them up in this upon a stove a few minutes, and pour a small ladle of broth, with a bit of butter mixt with flour; let all stew a quarter of an hour, take out your herbs, have ready a liaison as before, and just before your dinner-time pour it in, move it gently over the stove a minute, squeeze in an orange or lemon, and dish it up.

Ingredients

A small bunch of parsley, stalks and leaves separated

1 blade of mace

A sprig of thyme

100ml Champagne or white wine

400g small mushrooms

6-8 spring onions, sliced finely

Salt and pepper

20g butter mixed with 2 teaspoons of flour

100ml stock

A squeeze of lemon or orange juice

Method

1. Tie the parsley stalks in a bundle with the mace and thyme.

2. Put the Champagne or wine in a saucepan with the mushrooms, spring onions, bundle of herbs, and seasoning.

3. Simmer for 5 minutes then remove the bundle of herbs.

4. Add the butter and flour mixture then add the stock and stir as it thickens.

5. Cook gently for 15 minutes.

6. Add a squeeze of lemon or orange juice and the chopped parsley leaves.

Onions to Butter.

John Nott. 1723. 'The Cook and Confectioner's Dictionary.'

Peel them, put them into boiling Water, boil them well, drain them in a Colander, and butter them whole with boil'd Currans, Sugar, and beaten Cinnamon; serve them up on Sippets, strew fine Sugar over them, and run them over with beaten Butter.

Ingredients

12 small onions or shallots, peeled

40g butter

60g currants or sultanas

1 teaspoon of cinnamon

2 teaspoons of sugar

1 teaspoon of salt

Sippets or fingers of fried bread

Method

1. Boil the onions or shallots in salted water for 15 minutes then drain.

2. Melt the butter in a frying pan and add the onions or shallots, currants or sultanas, cinnamon, sugar and salt and fry gently for 5-10 minutes.

3. Serve with fried bread.

Note: I use small onions or shallots in this, so that they can be kept whole.

I didn't boil the currants or sultanas as they were already moist.

Onions in Ragou.

Spices were expensive, so they were often adulterated. The cookery writer, William Kitchiner, warned that imported cayenne pepper was not as reliable as home-grown varieties. He quoted Accum, a chemist working in London, whose publication 'A Treatise on Adulteration of Food and Culinary Processes' claimed that certain *'respectable shops in London'* sold cayenne that contained lead. Kitchiner also felt that imported cayenne was likely to be too hot, being *'an indiscriminate mixture of the powder of the dried pods of many species of capsicums, especially of the bird pepper, which is the hottest of all.'* He recommended the use of English chillies, which *'may be pounded in a deep mortar without any danger.'*

Ingredients

600g small onions or shallots, peeled

70g butter (reduced amount)

1 tablespoon of flour

200ml stock (reduced amount)

1 teaspoon of cayenne pepper

1 teaspoon of salt

1 teaspoon of mustard

25g breadcrumbs

Note: the word 'gravy' was used in a variety of ways, most commonly to mean stock or the juices from a piece of meat.

Richard Briggs. 1788. 'The English Art of Cookery.'

Peel a pint of small button onions, take four large ones, peel them, and chop them small; put a quarter of a pound of butter into a stew-pan, when it is melted and done making a noise put in the onions, and fry them of a nice brown, put in a little flour, and shake them round till they are thick; then put in half a pint of gravy, a little Cayan pepper and salt, a tea spoonful of mustard, and shake the pan round; when they are thick and well tasted put them in a dish, and garnish with fried crumbs of bread.

Method

1. Chop the four largest onions or shallots and halve the rest.

2. Melt 50g butter in a frying pan and add the onions or shallots.

3. Fry until golden then stir in the flour. Stir for a few minutes then add the stock. Stir the sauce as it thickens then add the cayenne pepper, salt and mustard. Put them in a serving dish and keep warm.

4. Fry the breadcrumbs in the remaining butter and sprinkle this over the dish.

To stew Peas after the French Fashion.

This recipe shows the influence of French food, which was very popular among the wealthy. Some felt that French cuisine was over elaborate and snobbish, and
the diarist Parson Woodforde complained that many dishes were *'spoiled by being so frenchified in dressing…'* (1985. 'A Country Parson: James Woodforde's Diary 1759-1802.')

John Nott. 1723. 'The Cook and Confectioner's Dictionary.'

Cut Lettuce into little bits, and also two or three onions, take some Butter and slices of Bacon, season these with Salt and whole Pepper, and toss them up in a stew pan till the Lettuce is hot; then put in the peas, and let them stew till they are tender; then add to them some good Broth or boiling Water, and let them stew again gently; broil a piece of Bacon and lay in the middle of the Dish with grated Bread and some Parsley; pour in your Soop, &c. and serve it up

Ingredients

30g butter

100g streaky bacon, chopped

2 onions, chopped

1 head of crisp lettuce e.g. Romaine, chopped

300g peas (fresh or frozen), cooked

50ml stock

Salt and pepper

A little parsley

50g breadcrumbs fried in 10g butter until golden (garnish)

Method

1. Melt the butter in a saucepan and fry the bacon and onions until golden. Set aside some of the bacon to use as a garnish.

2. Add the lettuce to the pan and fry until just softened. Season then add the peas and the stock and bring to a simmer.

3. Sprinkle over the bacon, fried breadcrumbs and a little parsley.

Note: this is good as a side dish but could become a main course if you put a piece of gammon in the middle, as described in the original recipe. If you add more stock, it becomes a soup.

Pease Pudding.

Sarah Martin. 1795. 'The New Experienced English-Housekeeper.'

Take split pease according to the size you would have your pudding, wash, pick them and tie them up in a cloth, take care to leave room for them to swell, and that no water gets in, put it into a pot and boil it two hours, then take it up and beat the pease small in a bowl, and add two ounces of butter, two eggs, two spoonsful of thick cream, a little salt and a little ground pepper, mix these well together, butter your cloth, tie it up as close as you can, and boil it an hour or more, these ingredients serve for a small pudding only.

Ingredients

150g split peas, soaked and rinsed

750ml stock or water

50g butter at room temperature

50ml double cream

2 eggs

Salt and pepper

2 teaspoons of grated nutmeg

Mint leaves, to decorate

Method

1. Cook the peas in the stock or water over a low heat (half covered with a lid) for 2 hours until thick and soft, and the liquid has been absorbed. Stir regularly to make sure it does not stick to the bottom of the pan.

2. Blend the peas with the butter, cream, eggs and seasoning.

3. Line a heat-proof bowl (about 16cm across) with cling-film and oil this thoroughly. Pour in the mixture, and fold the cling-film over the top. Cover with foil.

4. Cook on top of a double boiler or over a pan of boiling water for 2 hours.

5. Turn the pudding out carefully onto a plate and garnish with a few mint leaves.

Note: the diarist Parson Woodforde blamed his piles on eating too much pease pudding! (1985. 'A Country Parson: James Woodforde's Diary 1759-1802.')

Potato Balls Ragoût.

Kitchiner tested all of his recipes himself then submitted them to his 'Committee of Taste', '*composed of some of the most illustrious gastropholists of this luxurious metropolis*,' at dinners held weekly at his home in Camden. People were told to arrive at 7.00 and leave at 11.00, and if they were late they were not admitted. He greatly admired the French, both in terms of their culinary skills, and in the rather misguided belief that they did not get as drunk as the British: ' *their elastic stomachs, unimpaired by spirituous liquors, digest vigorously the food they sagaciously prepare and render easily assimilable, by cooking it sufficiently, wisely contriving to get half the work of the stomach done by fire and water.*'

Ingredients

450g potatoes, peeled

100g ham, finely chopped

4 tablespoons of the leaves of herbs such as tarragon, chives or parsley, chopped finely

2 shallots, chopped finely

2 egg yolks

Finely grated nutmeg

Salt and pepper

2 tablespoons flour

2 eggs, beaten

100g freshly made breadcrumbs

Butter or oil for frying

William Kitchiner. 1830. 'The Cook's Oracle.'

Are made by adding to a pound of (mashed) potatoes a quarter of a pound of grated ham, or some sweet herbs, or chopped parsley, an onion or eschalot, salt, pepper, and a little grated nutmeg, or other spice, with the yelk of a couple of eggs: roll them into balls; flour them, or egg and bread-crumb them; and fry them in clean drippings, or brown them in a Dutch oven. Obs.—An agreeable vegetable relish, and a good supper-dish.

Method

1. Boil the potatoes then mash them (or put them through a potato ricer).

2. Mix the potatoes with the ham, herbs, shallot, egg yolk, nutmeg and seasoning.

3. Form the mixture into balls.

4. Put the seasoned flour on one plate, the beaten egg in a bowl and the breadcrumbs on another plate.

5. Roll each potato ball in the flour, then the egg and then the breadcrumbs.

6. Heat the butter or oil (or a mixture of both) in a frying pan and gently fry the potato balls until golden on all sides.

Note: This makes 12-15 potato balls.

Potatoes Full Dressed.

Parson Woodforde recorded in his diary that: *'Robert Biggen for stealing Potatoes was this afternoon whipp'd thro' the streets of Cary by the Hangman at the end of a Cart. He was whipped from the George Inn to the Angel, from thence back thro' the street to the Royal Oak in South Cary and so back to the George Inn.'* (1759-1802)

William Kitchiner. 1830. 'The Cook's Oracle.'

The vegetable kingdom affords no food more wholesome, more easily procured, easily prepared, or less expensive, than the potato: yet, although this most useful vegetable is dressed almost every day, in almost every family, for one plate of potatoes that comes to table as it should, ten are spoiled. Wash them, but do not pare or cut them, unless they are very large. Fill a sauce-pan half full of potatoes of equal size (or make them so by dividing the larger ones), put to them as much cold water as will cover them about an inch: they are sooner boiled, and more savoury, than when drowned in water. Most boiled things are spoiled by having too little water, but potatoes are often spoiled by too much: they must merely be covered, and a little allowed for waste in boiling, so that they may be just covered at the finish.

It will be an elegant improvement ... previous to frying or broiling the potatoes, to flour them and dip them in the yelk of an egg, and then roll them in fine-sifted bread-crumbs; they will then deserve to be called POTATOES FULL DRESSED.

Ingredients

500g potatoes

20g flour with salt and pepper

2 egg yolks or 1 egg, beaten

100g fresh breadcrumbs

20g butter

2 tablespoons oil

Method

1. Boil the potatoes in their skins, drain them then allow them to cool.

2. Remove the skin from the potatoes then slice them fairly thickly. Dip each slice in the seasoned flour, then the egg and then the breadcrumbs.

3. Heat the butter and oil in a large frying pan over a medium heat. Fry the potatoes in batches, keeping them warm in an ovenproof dish in a low oven (around 120°c, gas 1).

Potatoe Pudding.

Baked puddings like this were often baked beneath spit-roast meat, so that the juices dripped down onto it, making it even more delicious.

Hannah Glasse, 1747. 'The Art of Cookery.'

Boil two pounds of potatoes, and beat them in a mortar fine, beat in half a pound of melted butter, boil it half an hour, pour melted butter over it, with a glass of white-wine, or the juice of a Seville orange, and throw sugar all over the pudding and dish.

Ingredients

900g potatoes, peeled

50ml white wine or freshly squeezed orange juice

125g butter at room temperature

Salt and pepper

2 tablespoons of sugar

Method

1. Boil the potatoes then drain them. Return them to the pan with the wine or orange juice, 100g butter and seasoning.

2. Mash these together then continue to cook over a very low heat for about 15 minutes until smooth and thickened, stirring regularly to make sure it doesn't stick to the bottom of the pan.

3. Melt the remaining 25g butter. Brush some over the base of an ovenproof dish (about 26 x 20cm). Sprinkle with one tablespoon of sugar.

4. Put the potato mixture into the dish and pour over the rest of the butter. Sprinkle over the remaining tablespoon of sugar and serve.

5. If you have made this in advance, you can heat it in the oven at 180°c, gas 4, for 20-30 minutes

Note: I tried this with the full amount of butter as in the original recipe, but it was much too fatty. The reduced amount works well, and is still lovely and buttery.

Potatoe Salad.

Ingredients

300g new potatoes, scraped, boiled and sliced

2 – 4 anchovies, chopped, or a teaspoon of anchovy essence

Salad sauce (below)

Optional: 50g olives, sliced, 2 teaspoons capers, chopped, lettuce or watercress

Salad Sauce.

Ingredients

2 egg yolks

Half a teaspoon of sugar

2 tablespoons of vinegar

A pinch of salt

4 tablespoons of oil

John Farley. 1792. 'The London Art of Cookery.'

The potatoes being boiled and skinned, cut them into thin slices, and pour over them the sauce usually eaten with common salads, adding a little essence of anchovy, or anchovy liquor.

Method

1. While the potatoes are still warm, pour over the salad sauce and mix in the anchovies.

2. Mix in the olives and capers, if using.

3. Just before serving add some lettuce or watercress if you like.

Note: I have added some extra ingredients, taken from 'a grand sallet for the spring' by John Nott, in 'The Cook and Confectioner's Dictionary', 1723. He suggested some unusual ingredients for salads: *'take Cowslip Buds, Violet-flowers and Leaves; young Lettuce, Spinage, Alexander Buds, Strawberry-leaves, Water-cresses ... then take also Capers, Olives, Samphire, Cucumbers, Broom-buds, Raisins, and Currans parboil'd, Almonds blanch'd, Barberries, and other Pickles;'*

His suggestion for a sauce was ' a little Salt, one part Mustard, two parts Vinegar, and three parts Oil, *well beaten together and poour'd over the Sallad, or put in, the several Sides of the Dish, that each Person may roll his Sallad in as he pleases.'*

John Farley. 1792. 'The London Art of Cookery.'

Take the yolks of two raw eggs, add a salt-spoonful of powdered lump sugar, mix together, and add by degrees four spoonsful of salad oil, mixing it very well the whole time: to these put best vinegar and salt, to the palate.

Method

Mix the egg yolks with the vinegar, salt and sugar then gradually add the oil, blending all the time. You can do this in a mini blender.

Note: this is a light mayonnaise.

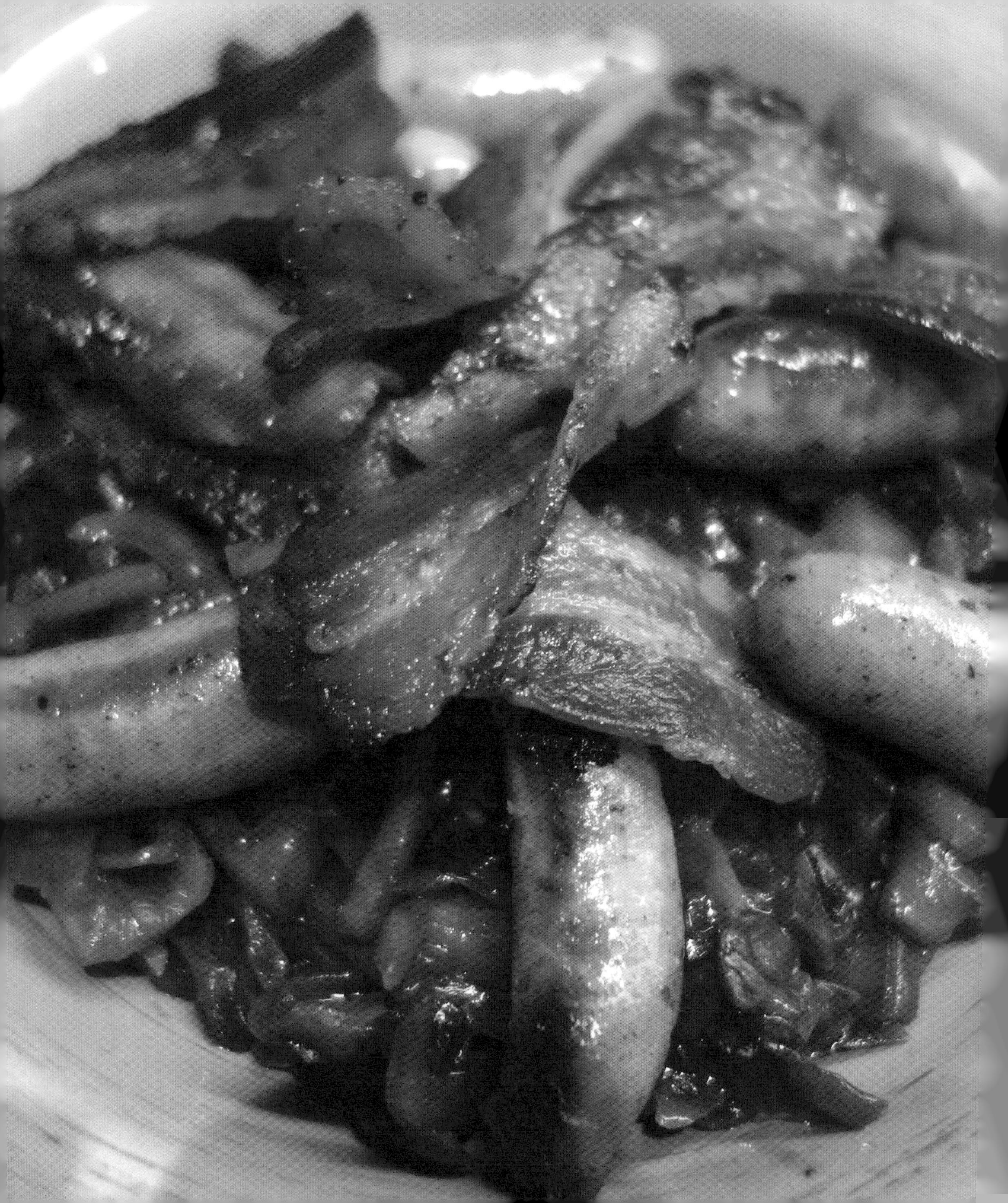

Red Cabbage Stewed.

Charlotte Mason. 1773. 'The Lady's Assistant.'

Take a fine red cabbage, cut it into thin slices cross-ways, and then into small bits; put them into a stew-pan, with a pint of rich gravy, a pound of sausages, and three or four slices of ham or bacon; cover up the stew-pan down close; set it on a moderate fire, let it stand half an hour, then uncover it; scum off the fat, shake in some flower, put in two spoonfuls of vinegar, and cover it up; set it on again, and let it stew four or five minutes longer; take out the sausages, and pour the rest over it.

Ingredients

(I have used approximately half of the quantities in the original recipe)

225g sausages, twisted in the middle and cut in half

4 rashers of streaky bacon, cut in half

300g red cabbage, shredded

1 level tablespoon flour

200ml stock (reduced quantity)

1 tablespoon of red wine vinegar

Salt and pepper

Method

1. Fry the sausages and bacon until crisp and golden. Remove from the pan and keep warm.

2. Fry the cabbage for about 10 minutes in the same frying pan, stirring it into the juices from the bacon and sausages. If necessary, add a little more butter.

3. Add the flour then stir around for a couple of minutes. Add the stock and vinegar and stir as it thickens. Simmer gently for about 30 minutes, then season.

4. Put the cabbage in a dish and arrange the sausages and bacon over it.

Note: I prefer to cook the bacon and sausages first rather than boiling them with the cabbage as the original recipe suggests. The caramelisation process gives them more flavour and a better colour.

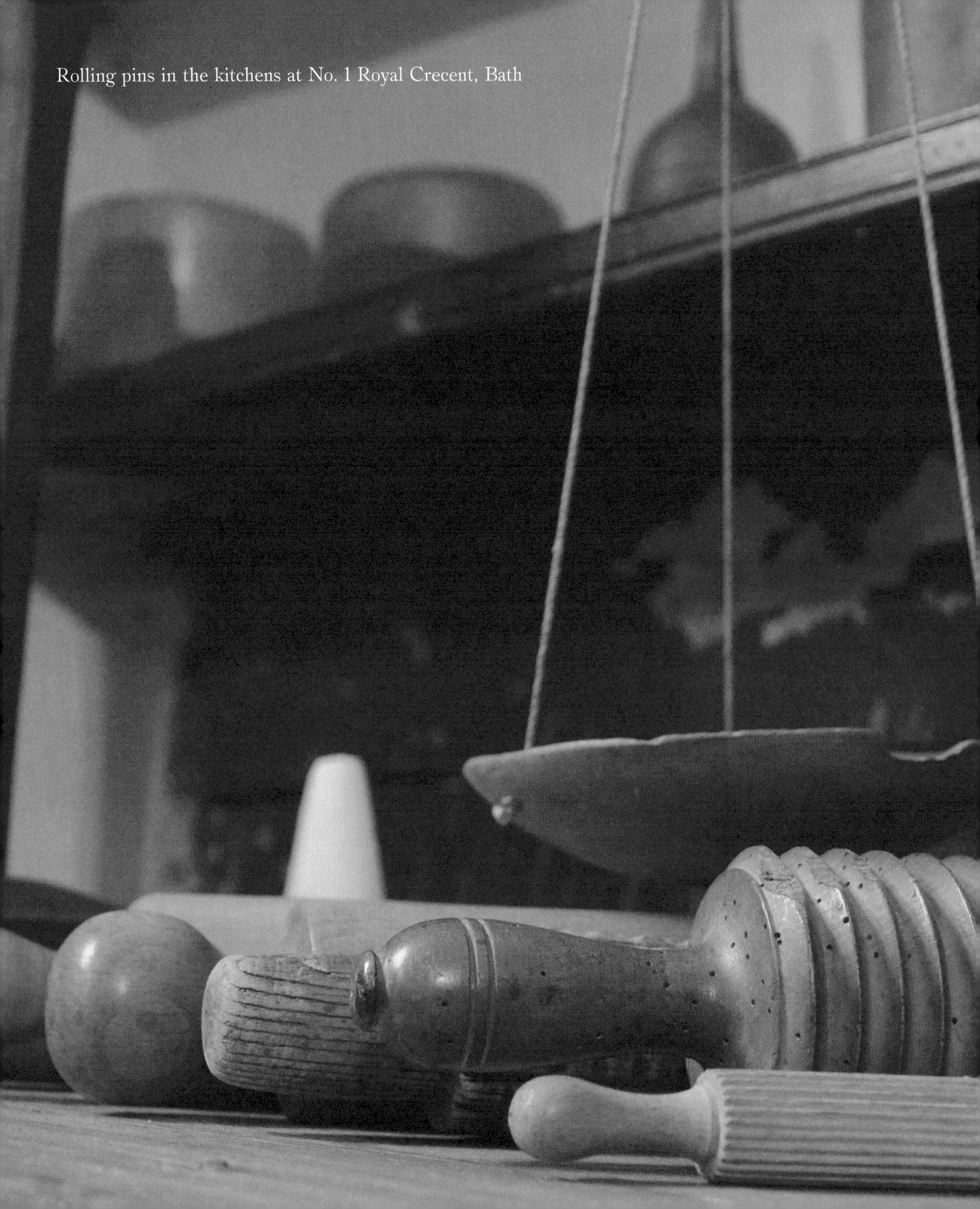

Rolling pins in the kitchens at No. 1 Royal Crecent, Bath

Sweet Dishes

'All the geniuses of the age are employed in designing new plans for dessert.'

Horace Walpole. 1753. 'The Letters of Horace Walpole.'

Sweet dishes were served as part of both the first and the second course. On special occasions these could be followed by the dessert course, by which time people would be very full. For this reason it was important to create beautiful, delicate dishes to tempt their appetites.

William Kitchiner, the cookery writer, mocked this excess: *'served up merely to feed the eye, or pamper palled appetite, that overcome the stomach and paralyze digestion, and seduce children of a larger growth to sacrifice the health and comfort of several days, for the baby-pleasure of tickling their tongue for a few minutes, with trifles and custards!!!'* (1817. 'The Cook's Oracle and Housekeeper's Manual.')

Home-grown fruit such as apples and pears were used to create sweet dishes. In Jane Austen's 'Emma', Mr. Woodhouse loved traditional dishes such as apple tart and custard, although his real favourite was a simple basin of gruel. (1815)

Aspirational families liked to serve more exotic fruits. At Pemberley, the ladies were served *'beautiful pyramids of grapes, nectarines and peaches.'* (1813. Jane Austen. 'Pride and Prejudice')

The popularity of these fruits led to some creative innovations. Hot-houses with furnaces made it possible to grow pineapples, grapes, peaches, figs and melons.

In Croome Park in Worcestershire there is a very grand 'temple greenhouse', Robert Adam's first garden building, with under-floor heating. Queen Charlotte described the exotic fruit served at a supper in St. George's Hall, after a ball. *'The dessert comprehended all that the hothouse could afford, and indeed more than it was thought art could have produced at that season. There was a profusion of pines, strawberries, peaches, nectarines, apricots, cherries of every kind, plums and raspberries.'* (1819. 'Memoirs of Queen Charlotte'.)

Those who lived in the cities could not grow their own fruit and had to visit the local markets. Tobias Smollett warned of the condition of the fruit in Covent Garden which was *'distributed by such filthy hands, as I cannot look at without loathing. It was but yesterday that I saw a dirty barrow-bunter in the street, cleaning her dusty fruit with her own spittle;'* (1771. 'Humphrey Clinker.')

Some Italian cooks, such as Jarrin the famous confectioner, came to England and opened ice cream shops. Jarrin described the process: *'To make ices, you must have a tub, or pail, in which you place your freezing-pot in the midst of pounded ice, well mixed with salt; the mixing of the salt with the ice must be particularly attended to, as upon this circumstance depends the freezing power, and consequently, in a great measure, the goodness of the ice.'* (1820. 'The Italian Confectioner')

Apple Cream.

John Nott. 1723. 'The Cook and Confectioner's Dictionary.'

Take a dozen Pippins, pare them, core them, cut them into thin Slices, and stew them in a Pipkin with red Wine, fine Sugar scraped, Lemon Peel and sliced Ginger, when they are very tender, put them in a Dish, and let them cool; boil a Quart of Cream with a little Nutmeg, and put some of the Apples among it, and sprinkle it with Rose-water and Sugar.

Ingredients

(I halved the quantities in the original recipe)

6 eating apples (about 500g), peeled, cored and sliced

50ml red wine (you can also use white wine, but the colour is less rosy!)

25g caster sugar plus one tablespoon to sprinkle on the top

Zest of half a lemon

1 teaspoon of grated fresh ginger

600ml double cream

Half a teaspoon of ground nutmeg

2 teaspoons of rose water

Method

1. Cook the apples in the wine with the sugar, lemon zest and ginger until the apples are soft and the wine has evaporated.

2. Put the cream, nutmeg and rose water into a saucepan and bring to the boil.

3. Pour the cream into the pan with the apples. Cover and leave to cool.

4. Tip the mixture into a serving bowl then sprinkle a little sugar over the top and chill.

Note: a pippin is an apple, and a pipkin is a cooking pot

This seems like an awful lot of cream, but it thickens up beautifully to produce a luscious, rich dessert.

Beggar's Pudding.

Sarah Harrison. 1733.'The House-Keeper's Pocket-Book; and Compleat Family Cook.'

Take some stale Bread; pour over it some hot Water, till it is well soaked; then press out the Water, and wash the Bread; add some powdered Ginger, Nutmeg grated, and a little Salt; some Rose Water or Sack, some Lisbon Sugar, and some Currants; mix these well together, and lay it in a Pan well buttered on the Sides; and when it is well flatted with a Spoon, lay some Pieces of Butter on the Top; bake it in a gentle Oven, and serve it hot. You may turn it out of the Pan when it is cold, and it will eat like a fine Cheesecake.

Ingredients

120g slices of white bread, crusts removed

60g sultanas

3 teaspoons of ground ginger

1 teaspoon of grated nutmeg

A pinch of salt

4 tablespoons of sherry, or a teaspoon of rose water mixed with some water, if you prefer

30g caster sugar plus a tablespoon for sprinkling

25g butter

Method

1. Soak the bread in hot water for about 30 minutes. Squeeze the water out then mix the bread with the sultanas, ginger, nutmeg, salt, sherry and sugar.

2. Use some of the butter to grease a small ovenproof dish (18x13cm) and pour in the mixture. Level the top then dot with the remaining butter. Sprinkle over the sugar then cook at 180°c, gas 4, for about 30 minutes until golden and crisp on top.

Note: this is like a bread and butter pudding but without the cream. It is quite plain but the sherry and sultanas definitely improve the taste. It is also good served with cream, of course.

It is interesting that this recipe contains sherry, probably as a form of comfort for the poor.

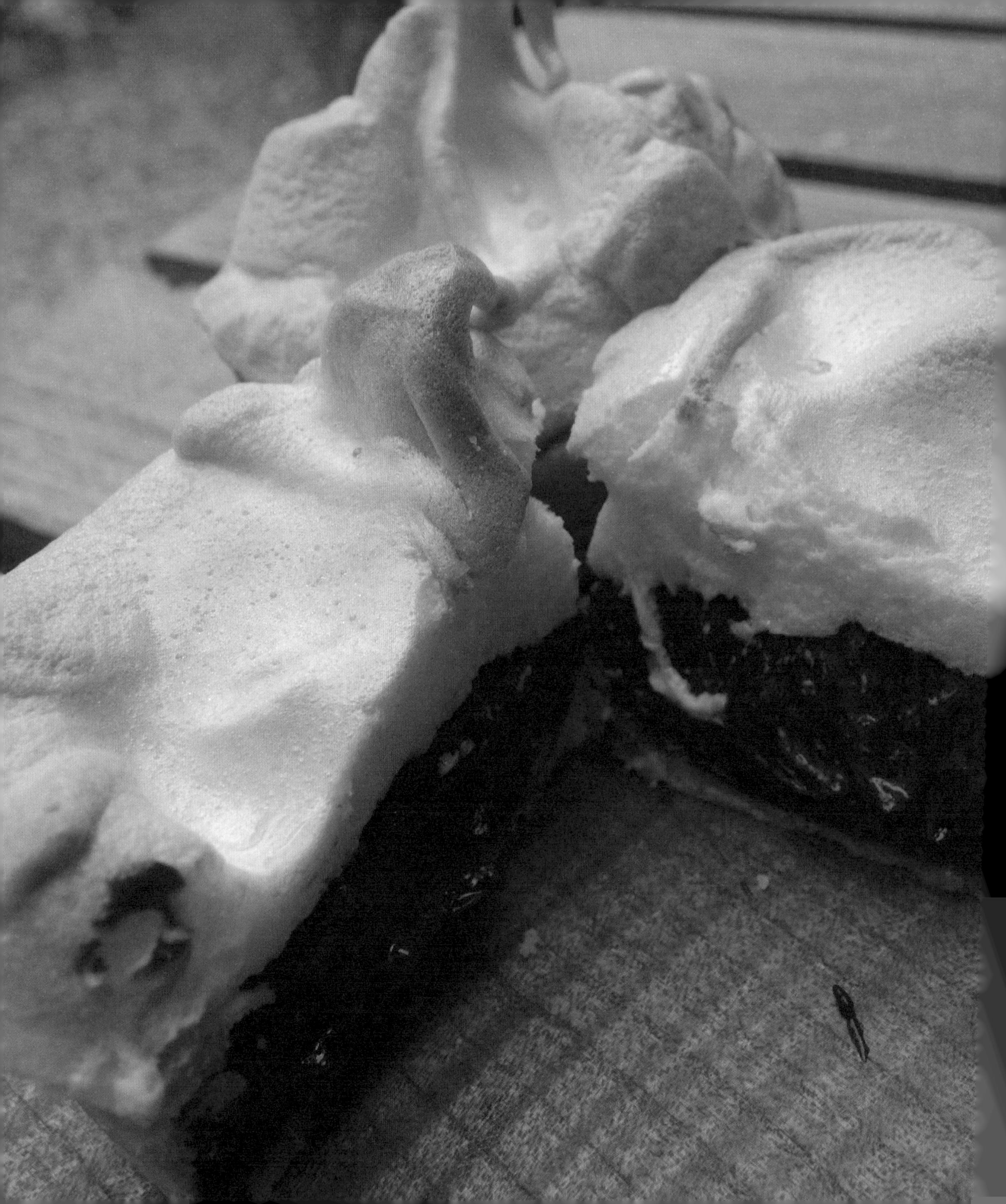

Chocolate Tart.

During the Georgian period some chocolate came from Sri Lanka and Ghana, where slave labour was common. For this reason it was boycotted by those fighting against slavery.

Charlotte Mason. 1773. 'The Lady's Assistant.'

Take a quarter of a pound of rasped chocolate, a stick of cinnamon, some fresh lemon-peel grated, a little salt, and some sugar; take two spoonfuls of fine flower, the yolks of six eggs well beat and mixed with some milk; put all these into a stew-pan, and let them be a little while over the fire; then put in a little preserved lemon-peel cut small, and let it stand to be cold; beat up the whites of eggs, enough to cover it, put it in puff-paste: when it is baked, sift some sugar over it, and glaze it with a salamander.

Ingredients

100ml milk

100g good quality dark chocolate, grated

1 teaspoon of ground cinnamon

The zest of 1 lemon, grated finely

25-50g preserved or pickled lemon, chopped fine - about a quarter of a lemon. (See Charlotte Mason's recipe in the section on 'Preserves')

100g caster sugar

3 eggs, separated

2 teaspoons flour

Puff pastry

Method

1. Gently warm the milk in a pan then add the chocolate, cinnamon, lemon zest, preserved lemon and half the sugar. Stir briefly to melt the chocolate then add the egg yolks mixed with the flour. Cook gently for a few minutes, stirring to thicken, but do not let it simmer as this would spoil the chocolate. Allow to cool.

2. Whisk the egg whites until fairly stiff then gradually add the remaining sugar, still whisking, to make a meringue mixture.

3. Butter a tart tin with a removable base and dust it with flour.

4. Roll out the pastry as thin as you can and use it to line the tin.

5. Pour the chocolate filling into the pastry case then top with the meringue mixture.

6. Bake in the oven at 180°c, gas 4, for 25-30 minutes

Note: this is an unusual recipe as it uses pickled lemon. It can either be made as a single tart, or as individual tarts (they take less time to cook.)

I left out the salt, as the preserved lemon is salty.

I added sugar to the whisked egg whites, but you may want to leave this out to be true to the original recipe, which simply sifts sugar over at the end. You can also fold the whisked egg whites (without added sugar) into the chocolate mixture then pour it into the pastry case and bake as before.

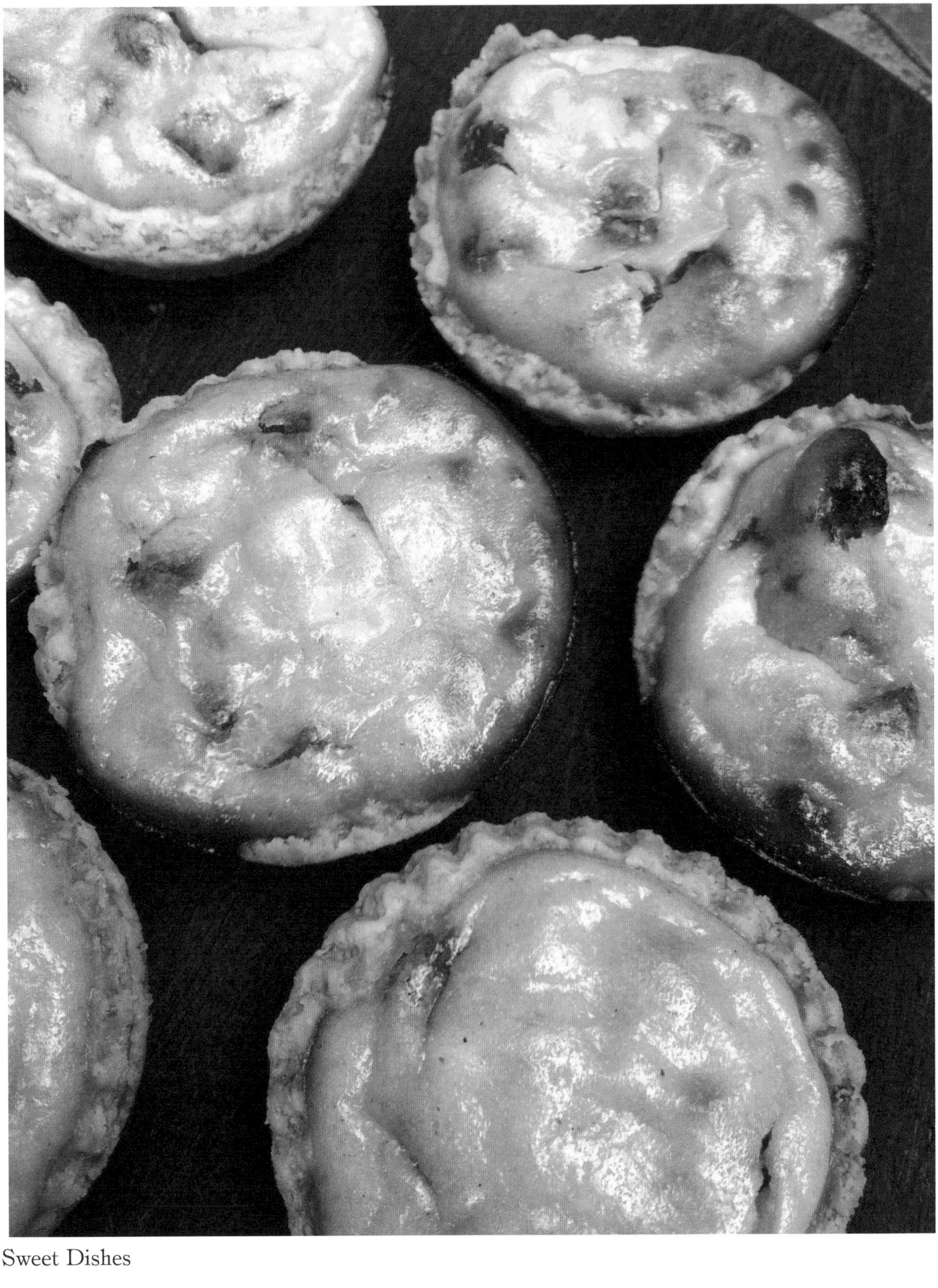

Curd Cheesecakes.

Charlotte Mason. 1773. 'The Lady's Assistant.'

Beat half a pint of good curd with four eggs, four spoonfuls of cream, some nutmeg, a little brandy, half a pound of currants; sugar to the taste; puff paste.

Ingredients

(I halved the quantities given in the original recipe; this fills 12-15 muffin / bun tins)

150g curd cheese or cream cheese

50g caster sugar

2 eggs, beaten

2 tablespoons of cream (about 40ml)

1 teaspoon of grated nutmeg

110g currants or sultanas

25ml brandy

Puff pastry

Method

1. Beat the curd cheese with the sugar in a bowl until creamy then add the eggs a little at a time.

2. Add the cream, nutmeg, currants or sultanas and brandy.

3. Roll out the pastry fairly thin and cut circles to fit your bun tins.

4. Butter the bun tins, dust them with flour and put in the circles of pastry.

5. Put the filling into the cases, making sure each one has some currants or sultanas then bake in the oven at 180°c, gas 4 for 25-30 minutes.

Note: if you have time, soak the currants or sultanas in the brandy; they will plump up and absorb the brandy.

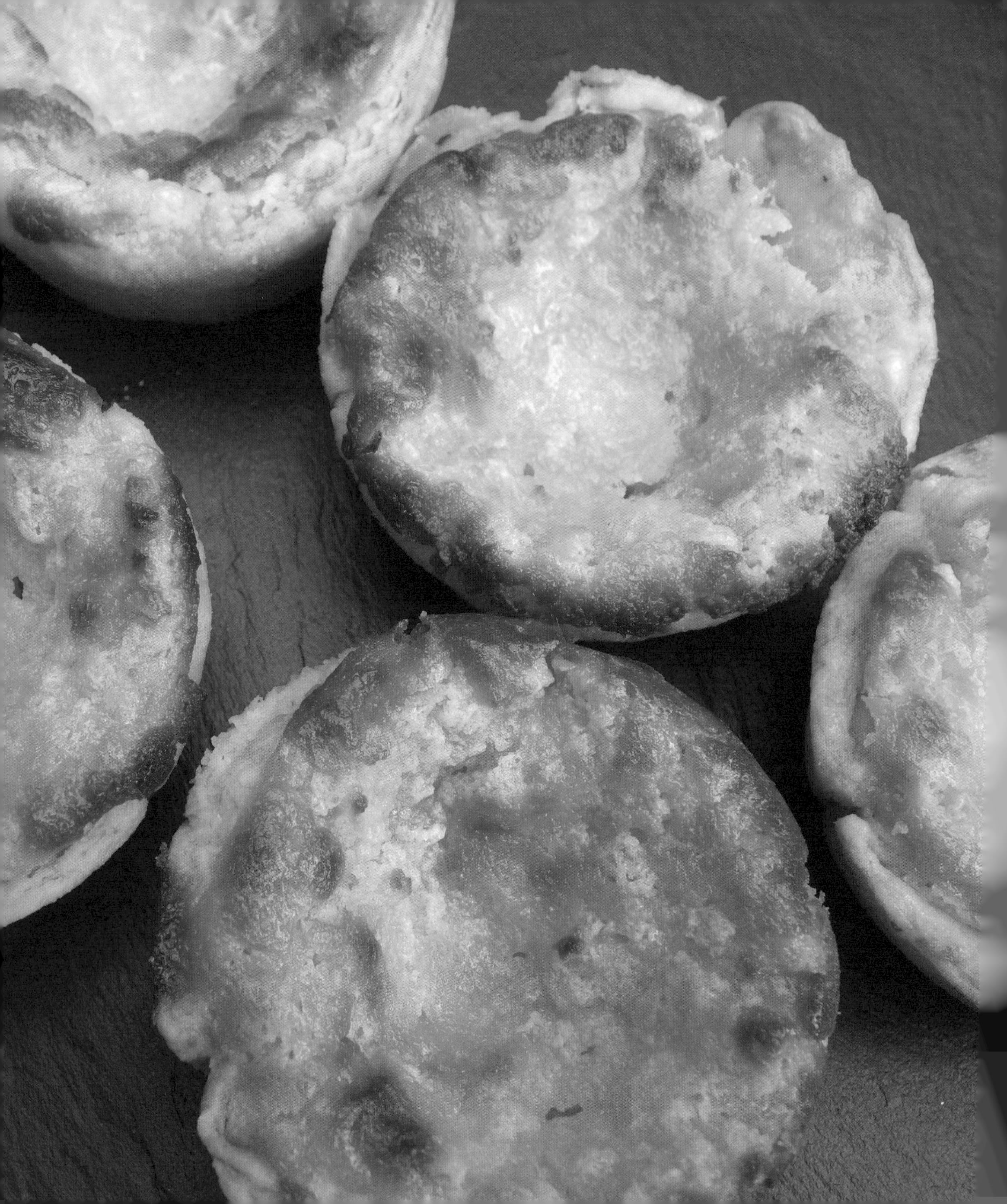

Lemon Cheesecakes.

'Loaf' sugar was chipped off a cone-shaped lump or loaf of sugar. This would be broken up, first using a hammer and chisel, then sugar 'nippers'. It could then be ground up in a mortar and pestle for use in cooking.

Hannah Glasse. 1747. 'The Art of Cookery Made Plain and Easy.'

Boil very tender the peel of two large lemons, and pound it well in a mortar, with a quarter of a pound of loaf sugar, the yolks of six eggs, half a pound of fresh butter, and a little curd beat fine. Pound and mix all together, lay a puff paste on the patty pans, fill them half full, and bake them. Orange cheesecakes are done the same way; but boil the peel in two or three waters, to deprive it of its bitter taste.

Ingredients

Zest of 2 lemons

100g caster sugar

225g butter, at room temperature

6 egg yolks

150g curd cheese or cream cheese

Puff pastry

Method

1. Put the lemon zest into a pan of boiling water then boil for a couple of minutes. Drain well.

2. Put the zest in a blender with the sugar. Blend until fine.

3. Beat the butter with the lemon zest and sugar then add the egg yolks, one at a time, beating continuously until smooth and creamy. Then add the curd cheese and mix until smooth.

4. Butter a tray of bun tins and dust them with flour.

5. Roll out the pastry and cut it into circles to fit your tins. Put a circle of pastry in each tin.

6. Fill the pastry cases with the lemon mixture and bake at 200°c, gas 6 for 15-20 minutes, until the filling is set and golden on top. Allow to cool before removing gently from the tins.

Note: this makes about 16 individual cheesecakes.

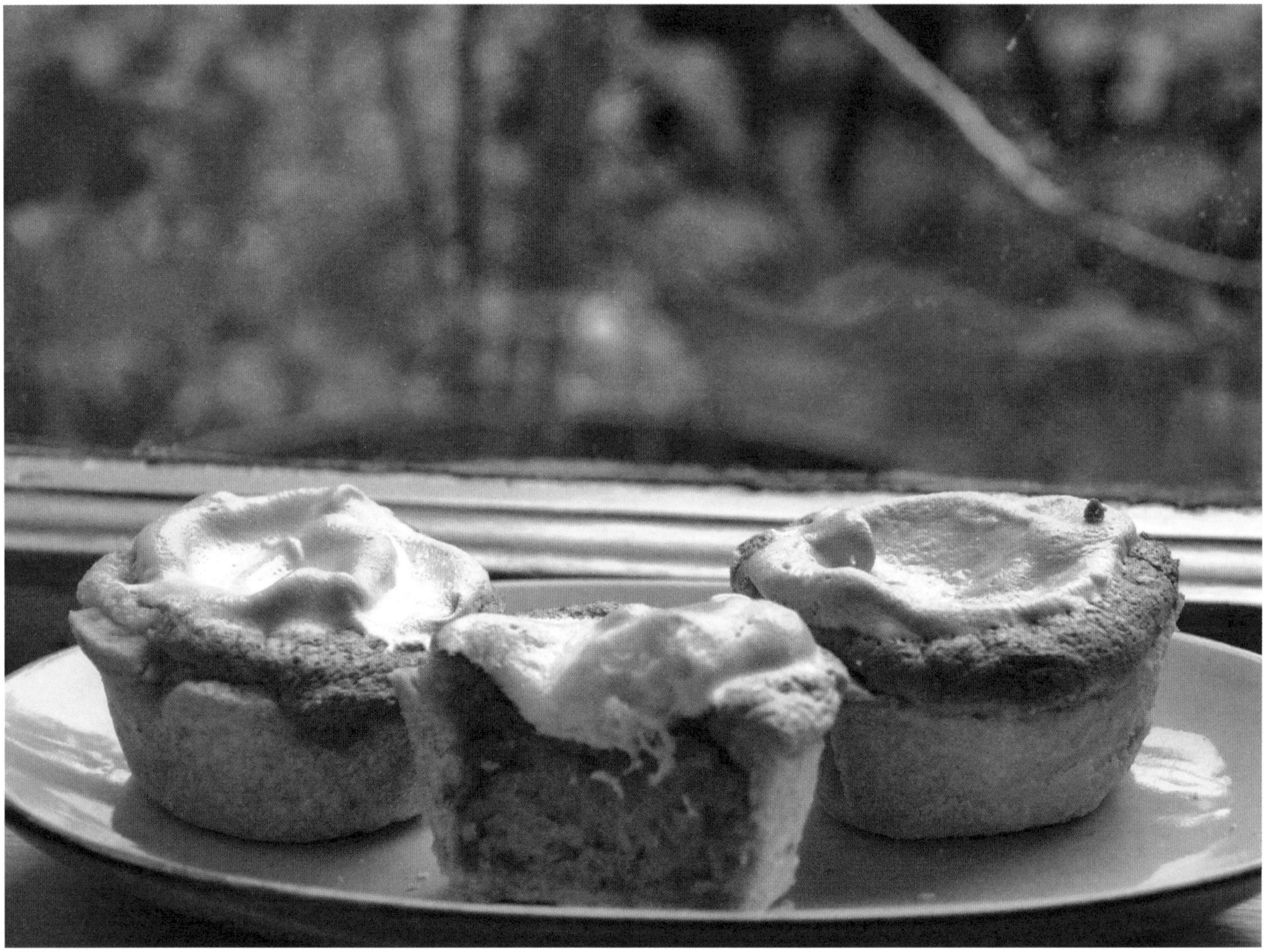

Orange Cheesecakes.

Robert Smith. 1723. 'Court Cookery.'

Blanch half a Pound of Almonds, beat them very fine, with Orange-Flower Water, half a Pound of fine Sugar beaten, that must be almost cold before you use it; then take ten Eggs, the Whites but of four, very well beaten, two Candied Orange-peels, or Raw with the Bitterness boil'd out; beat the Peels in a Mortar till as tender as Marmalade, without any Knots; then mix all well together.

For the Crust, take a Pound of the finest Flower, and three Ounces of refin'd Sugar, mix it with the Flower; then take half a Pound of fresh Butter, work it with your Hand till it comes to a Froth; then put in the Flower by Degrees, and work it together, in the Yolks of three Eggs, and the Whites of two: if it be Limber, put in more Flower and Sugar, till it's fit to roll out; then make them in what Form you please: A little above a quarter of an Hour bakes them. Against they come out of the Oven, have some refin'd Sugar, beat up with the White of an Egg, as thick as you can; then ice them all over, and set them in the Oven to harden again.

Ingredients

(I halved the quantities given in the original recipe)

110g almonds

1 tablespoon of orange flower water

110g caster sugar

100g candied orange peel (see recipe in the 'Preserves' section)

3 eggs and 2 egg yolks

Pastry:

225g plain flour

35g caster sugar

110g butter at room temperature

1 egg, beaten

Topping:

1 egg white

20g sifted icing sugar

Method

1. Put the almonds in a blender with orange flower water, sugar and the candied orange peel. Blend until smooth.

2. Whisk the eggs until creamy then add the orange and almond mixture, a spoonful at a time.

3. To make the pastry, mix the flour and the sugar then rub in the butter. Add the egg, and work to a paste.

4. Roll out the pastry and cut out circles. Butter 12 - 15 deep bun tins and dust them with flour. Press in the pastry circles.

5. Put the filling into the pastry cases and bake at 180°c, gas 4 for 12-15 minutes. The filling should be slightly risen and golden.

6. Whisk the egg white until stiff then whisk in the icing sugar until it is thick and brush this over the cheesecakes. Return them to the oven for a few minutes.

Note: this cheesecake does not contain any cheese, but the word was used to describe the texture rather than the content of the dish.

Orange Pudding.

Richard Briggs. 1788. 'The English Art of Cookery.'

Take the yolks of twelve and the whites of four eggs, and beat them well; put half a pound of butter into a stew-pan and melt it, put it to the eggs, and beat them well together; grate in the rind of two fine Seville oranges, half a pound of fine powdered sugar, a spoonful of orange-flower water, one of rose water, a gill of sack; and half a pint of cream, with two Naples biscuits soaked in it, mix all well together, and squeeze in the juice of one orange; lay puff-paste round the rim of the dish, put it in, and bake it; when it is done send it up hot to table.

Ingredients

(I halved the quantities given in the original recipe)

100g Naples biscuits (see 'Cakes' section) or use sponge biscuits

140ml sherry (originally called 'sack', from the French word 'sec', or 'dry'.)

300ml cream

4 eggs

8 egg yolks

225g icing sugar (sifted)

225g butter, melted

1 teaspoon of caraway seeds

1 teaspoon of orange flower water

1 teaspoon of rose water

2 oranges

Method

1. Soak the biscuits in the sherry and cream for at least 10 minutes then mash them to break them up.

2. Whisk the eggs and egg yolks with the sugar until thick and creamy. This takes some time, so it is best to use an electric whisk.

3. Stir in the melted butter, caraway seeds, orange flower water, rose water, orange zest and the juice of one orange.

4. Stir in the biscuit, sherry and cream mixture.

5. Pour the mixture into a buttered ovenproof dish (about 24 x 19cm) and bake at 170°c, gas 3, for 40-45 minutes. Serve hot.

Note: this is a batter pudding. You can add a puff pastry rim if you like (as in the original recipe), but I don't think it adds much to the flavour or appearance.

Pear Compote, with Wine.

Jarrin. 1820. 'The Italian Confectioner.'

Choose very ripe pears, peel them, and cut them in halves; put them in a silver pan, with a glass of good wine, and some pulverised sugar and cinnamon; let them broil, and reduce the syrup; when done, take them off, and put them into a silver compotier, and cover it with your pan to make them a fine colour.

Ingredients

100g caster sugar

100ml white or red wine

1-2 teaspoons of ground cinnamon, or 1 stick

500g pears, peeled and halved, with the core carefully removed

Method

1. Dissolve the sugar in the wine in a pan and add the cinnamon, then add the pears.

2. Simmer until the pears are tender and the liquid is syrupy – about 20 minutes (depending on the ripeness of the pears). Put the pears and their syrup in a jar, cover and store in the fridge.

Note: compotes were served up in special dishes called 'compotiers'. Placing a hot pan over it must have given the fruit a shine or glaze.

Raspberry Compote.

Jarrin. 1820. 'The Italian Confectioner.'

Choose some fine, clean, and ripe raspberries; wash them, boil some syrup to a blow, and put in the raspberries, and take them off again almost instantly, as they must not be suffered to boil. Leave them in the syrup four or five hours, put them on the fire again, and warm them till they are near boiling; after wards let them cool, and put them in your compotiers.

Ingredients

100ml water

100g caster sugar

300g raspberries

Method

1. Dissolve the sugar in the water then boil until it becomes syrupy (90 - 100°c).

2. Add the raspberries and then remove the pan from the heat. Leave for 4-5 hours then heat them until almost boiling. Remove them from the heat, and put them into a jar.

Note: Jarrin was an expert in the use of sugar and was famous for his decorative patisserie. He gave exact descriptions of each stage of boiling such as the 'blow' stage in this recipe:

Blow: May be known, by dipping the skimmer into the sugar, shaking it, and blowing through the holes: if, in doing this, sparks of light or bubbles be seen, we may be sure of the blow.

Ratafie Pudding.

Ratafia biscuits are like macaroons, made with almonds.

Nott suggested using a savoy cake mould, which was very decorative. You can make the pudding in a simple heatproof bowl, which is much simpler to turn out. The sauce makes it look lovely.

Ingredients

(I halved the quantities used in the original recipe)

300ml cream

300ml milk

Zest of a lemon

2 tablespoons of caster sugar

1 stick cinnamon

75g breadcrumbs

100-150g ratafia biscuits (see recipe in the 'Cakes' section)

50g dried cherries

5 large eggs, beaten

Wine sauce:

20g butter

2 teaspoons flour

100ml white wine

2 teaspoons of caster sugar

1 teaspoon of ground nutmeg

25ml brandy

Frederick Nutt. 1809. 'The Imperial and Royal Cookbook.'

Put a pint of milk and a pint of cream into a stewpan, with the peel of two lemons, a little cinnamon, and sugar; set it on the fire, and let it boil for half an hour; then strain it into a bason, and put the crumb of two French rolls into it; then butter a savoy-mould cake, and stick dry cherries according to fancy; then put in half a pound of ratifies in the mould; break ten eggs in the bason, beat them up well, then put the eggs to the boiled milk, cream, and rolls; stir it well, so as to blend the rolls, eggs, and milk, together; then put it in the mould that has the ratifies in: finish the same as the ginger soufflé *: pour wine sauce over it.

* put the mould into a stewpan that has boiling water that will come better than half way up the mould; cover the stewpan, and put lighted charcoal on the cover; keep it boiling very slow for an hour, or better; take the mould out of the stewpan about ten minutes before it is wanted, by which means the soufflé will keep firmer; before it is turned out of the mould run the knife round it, by way of loosening it. The wine sauce is made as follows: - put about an ounce of butter into a stewpan; when melted, put about half a table-spoonful of flour; stir it until it is mixed with the butter, then add white wine to it, to make it of the thickness of melted butter; grate a little nutmeg in it, and put about half a glass of brandy in the sauce

Method

1. Put the milk and cream in a pan with the lemon zest, sugar and cinnamon. Simmer very gently over a low flame for 30 minutes. Strain onto the breadcrumbs and leave to cool.

2. Butter a heat-proof bowl (about 1 litre in size). Line the dish with the biscuits and cherries.

3. Add the eggs to the cream mixture and pour this into the bowl. Cover and steam over a pan of hot water for 2 hours.

4. To make the wine sauce, melt the butter in a pan then stir in the flour. Cook gently then add the wine and stir to thicken. Add the sugar, nutmeg and brandy.

5. When the pudding has cooked, leave it to stand for 10 minutes then turn it out of its bowl and pour over the sauce.

Trifle.

Frederick Nutt. 1809. 'The Imperial and Royal Cook.'

Cut a few slices of savoy cake and put them at the bottom of a trifle dish, (which is something like a salad-dish, in respect to depth); lay a layer of macaroons on them, and a layer of ratifies; pour a pint of Lisbon over the cakes, leave it long enough to soak all the wine up, and then cover the cakes with custard, made in the following manner:-

Put a quart of milk and cream mixed, and a little cinnamon, lemon peel, and sugar; let it boil for half an hour; take if off the stove, and put it to cool: to this quantity of milk and cream put the yolks of eight eggs, and a spoonful of flour; beat them up in a bason, with a spoon, very well; put the milk in by little at a time, and keep stirring all the while; then strain it through a hair-sieve into a stewpan; put it on a brisk fire, and be sure to keep stirring it until it comes to a boil; then take it off, and put it to cool; when half cold, add a glass of brandy and a few spoonfuls of ratifee; then cover the cakes with it, and lay apricot jam upon the custard; then put a pint of good cream into a bason, with the white of an egg, a lump of sugar rubbed to a lemon, and about two glasses of white wine; beat it up with a whisk, and skim the froth with a spoon that has holes in it; lay the froth on the back of the sieve, which should be laid upon a dish, to save the drainings to be returned to the pan again, for whipping; lay the whipped cream over the trifle; put a few harlequin seeds in any form you think proper: garnish the edge of the dish with preserved orange, or dried orange peel.

Trifle was originally a kind of fool, made with sweetened cream and spices. By the Georgian era, sponge or biscuits soaked in wine or some form of alcohol were added, leading to variations whose name reflected the impact of the dessert, such as Tipsy Pudding or Whim Wham. The word 'trifle' means something of little significance, maybe because of an association with left-over cake or biscuits, but in fact it is a very rich dessert.

As time went on, recipes became increasingly grand and complex, like this one from Frederick Nutt, who was an aspirational cook, having served as an apprentice to the great Italian confectioner, Domenico Negri. He made it clear that his recipes were only for the affluent.

Method: see over.

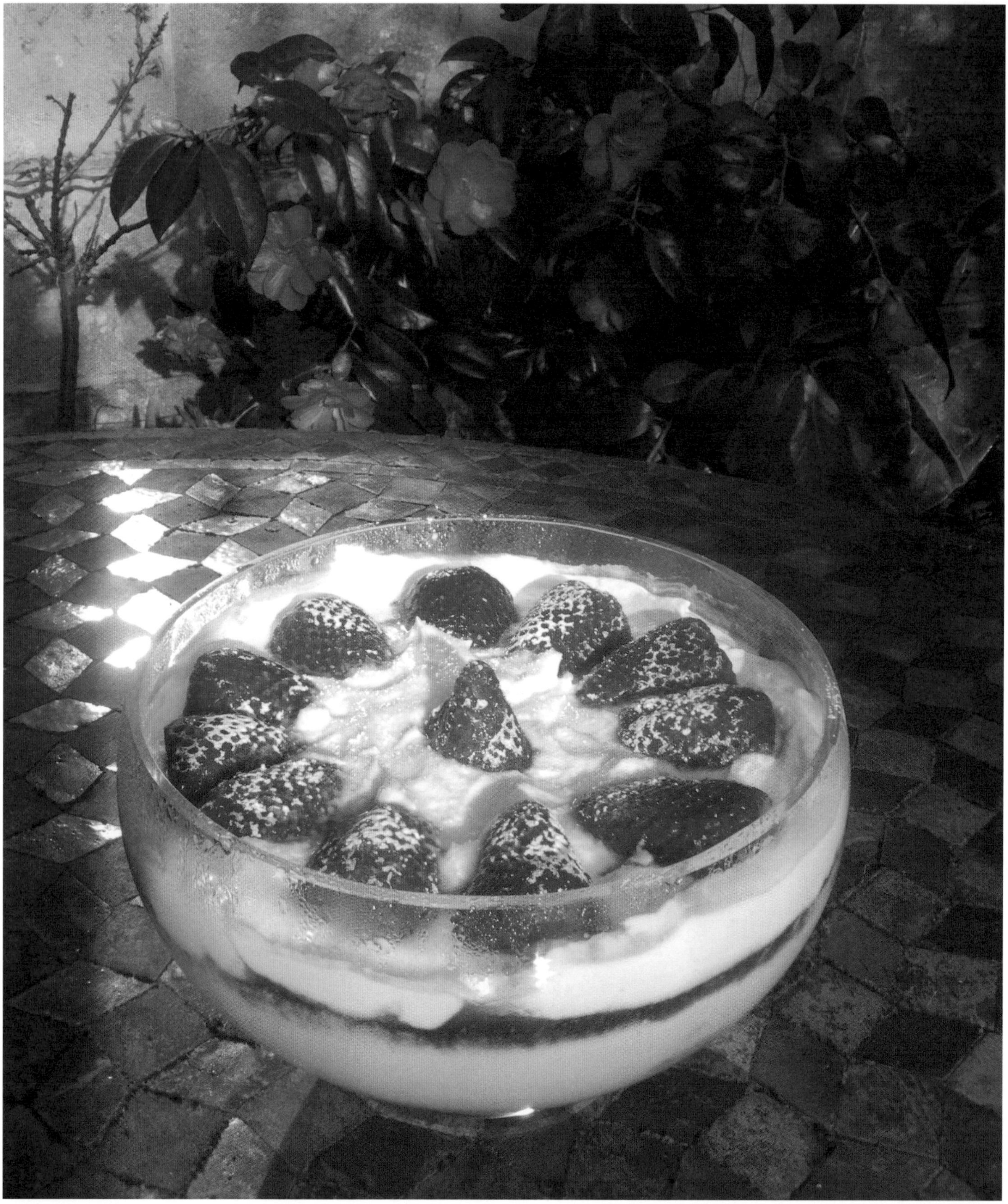

Trifle. Continued.

Ingredients

Note: this is a big trifle – enough for about 8 people.

250g savoy cake (this is a fairly hard, dry cake which is good for absorbing liquid. I have given a recipe in the "Cakes' section, but you can use any kind of plain sponge.)

200ml port or 'Lisbon' (alternatively you could use sherry or marsala)

200g macaroons and / or ratafias (there are recipes for these in the 'Cakes' section. You can substitute more cake if you don't like the taste of almonds)

Custard:

250ml double cream

250ml milk

1 stick of cinnamon

1 strip of lemon peel

100g caster sugar

4 egg yolks

2 teaspoons of cornflour

75ml brandy or 50ml brandy and 25ml ratafia (an orange brandy drink - see the section on 'Drinks')

Jam: 250ml jam – apricot, if you want to stick to the original recipe

Syllabub:

300ml double cream

100ml white wine

2 egg whites

10g caster sugar

Zest of a lemon

Topping:

Candied orange peel or lemon comfits (see recipes for these in the 'Preserves' section)

Method

1. Place the savoy cake at the bottom of a trifle dish. Pour over half the port.

2. Put a layer of macaroons and / or ratafias over this, then pour over the rest of the port and leave it until the liquid has all been soaked up.

3. To make the custard, put the cream and milk, cinnamon, lemon peel, and sugar into a pan and simmer for 20 - 30 minutes, until thickened.

4. Beat the egg yolks in a bowl with the cornflour then gradually pour in the cream and milk, mixing with a hand whisk. Pass this through a sieve into a clean pan and heat gently, whisking as it thickens. Add the brandy.

5. Pour the custard over the cake, and cover it. When it is cold, spread the jam over the custard (if it is not cold enough it is hard to spread the jam evenly).

6. To make the syllabub, whisk the cream until thick then gradually add the white wine. Whisk the egg whites until stiff then add the sugar a little at a time, whisking all the time. Gently combine the cream with the egg whites then stir in the lemon zest. Spread this over the top of the trifle. Chill.

7. Decorate with lemon comfits or candied orange peel.

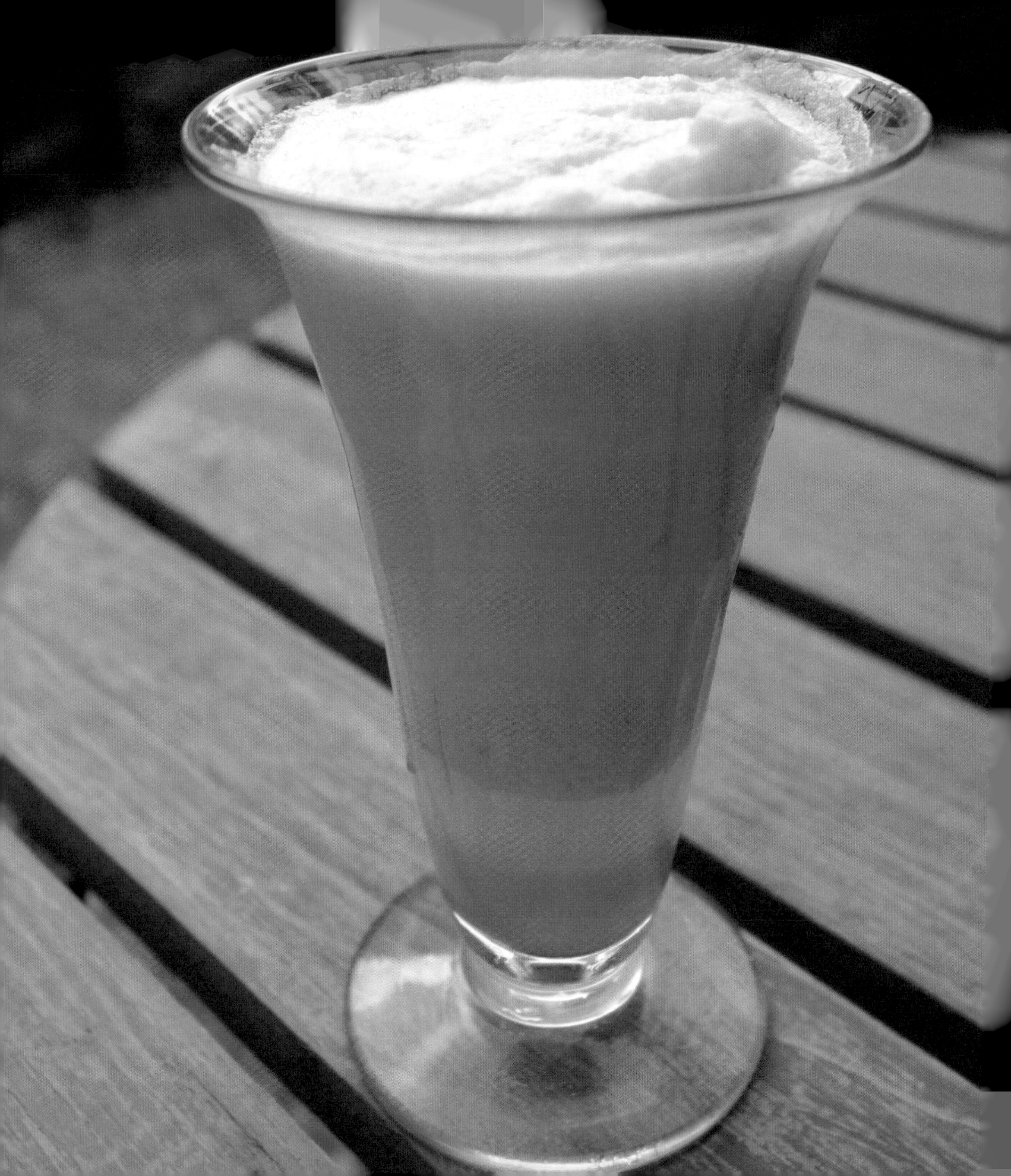

Whipp'd syllabub.

Cream was a popular ingredient in sweet dishes. There were dairies in the towns but they were not always very hygienic. The best were in the countryside, where some were designed to be so clean and attractive that they could be used for entertaining, especially at tea-time. Caroline Powys described Lady Leicester's dairy in Wesenham Hall as: *'the neatest place you can imagine.'* (1899. Passages from the Diaries of Mrs. Philip Lybbe Powys of Hardwick House: 1756-1808'.)

Tobias Smollet's character, Matt. Bramble, was filled with enthusiasm for his dairy, which he said: *'flows with nectar and tides of milk and cream, from whence we derive abundance of excellent butter, curds, and cheese'.* (1771. 'Humphrey Clinker')

Dairies were seen as emblematic of innocent rustic charm, so perhaps it seemed natural that when Sir Harry Fetherstonhaugh of Uppark House in West Sussex, heard his dairymaid, Mary Ann Bullock, sing, he should marry her. He was 70 and she was 21.

Henry Howard. 1703. 'England 's Newest Way in Cookery.'

Take a Pint of Cream, six spoonful of Sack, the Whites of two Eggs, three Ounces of fine Sugar, and with a Birch-twig beat it 'till it froth well; skim it and put it into your Syllabub-glasses.

Ingredients

(I halved the quantities used in the original recipe)

1 egg white

300ml cream

45g caster sugar

40-50ml sherry

Method

1. Whisk the egg white until fairly stiff but not dry.

2. Whisk the cream until just starting to thicken.

3. Add the sugar and sherry to the cream then fold in the egg whites.

Note: this is easy to make and does not separate, as some recipes for syllabub do.

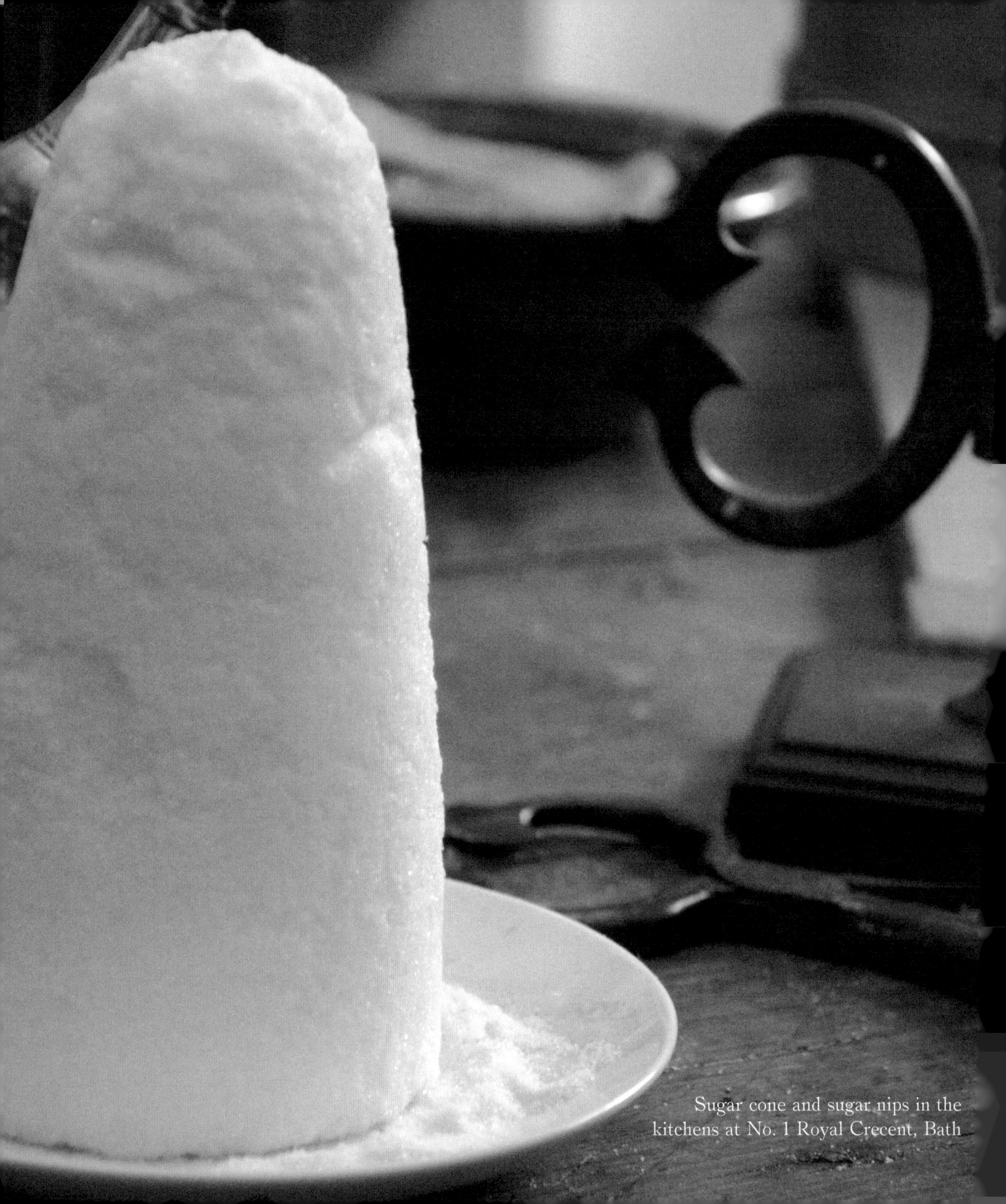

Sugar cone and sugar nips in the
kitchens at No. 1 Royal Crecent, Bath

Cakes and Biscuits.

'In the Morning my Quaker-Landlady came and visited us, before we were up, and made us eat Cakes, and drink Chocolate in-Bed.'

Daniel Defoe. 1724. 'Roxana'.

Sugar was a passion among the Georgians and every meal included something sweet and (hopefully) delicious. Sugar was produced in the West Indies on plantations, many of which had British landowners. The slaves were shipped to the colonies, and sugar, molasses, and rum were brought back to England. Many made their fortunes from the trade, establishing great houses and estates.

Others were horrified by accounts of the slave trade, such as Olaudah Equiano's 'Interesting Narrative'. He had been both slave and slave trader, so his descriptions of the dreadful conditions on slave ships were vivid. He said that some jumped overboard into the sea, preferring death to a life of slavery. He had experienced this kind of desperation himself: *'I called upon God's thunder, and his avenging power, to direct the stroke of death to me, rather than permit me to become a slave, and to be sold from lord to lord.'* (1789)

Pamphlets were produced that aimed to make people aware of the evils of slavery, and to persuade people to give up sugar and rum in protest. They pointed out that: *'the slave-dealer, the slave-holder, and slave-driver are virtually the agents of the consumer, and may be considered as employed and hired by him to procure the commodity.'* (1792. William Fox. 'An Address to the People of Great Britain, on the propriety of abstaining from West India sugar and rum'.)

Some protesters, known as 'anti-saccharites', refused to eat sugar until slavery had been abolished. At Harewood House in Yorkshire, sugar cane was grown in greenhouses, an experiment that impressed William Wilberforce, a leading figure in the anti-slavery movement in England.

Sugar was refined in England and made into cones, called 'loaf sugar'. Jarrin, the Italian Confectioner, said that it *'should be fine, white, dry, and difficult to break, and present a sparkling appearance when broken.'* (1820) Lumps were broken off for everyday use, but for cooking it was ground in a mortar and pestle.

Along with the import of sugar into London, Bristol and Liverpool, came a range of spices from the east. It became increasingly common to cook with these, and most kitchens would have had a store of them, kept in a box with separate divisions for each spice.

Francis Sykes, the youngest son of a Yorkshire farmer, became so wealthy as a result of working for the East India Company that he was able to buy Basildon Park in Berkshire. He had to return to England due to ill health, but brought with him some China with the crest of the 'Demi Lady of Bengal', to remind him of the country he clearly loved.

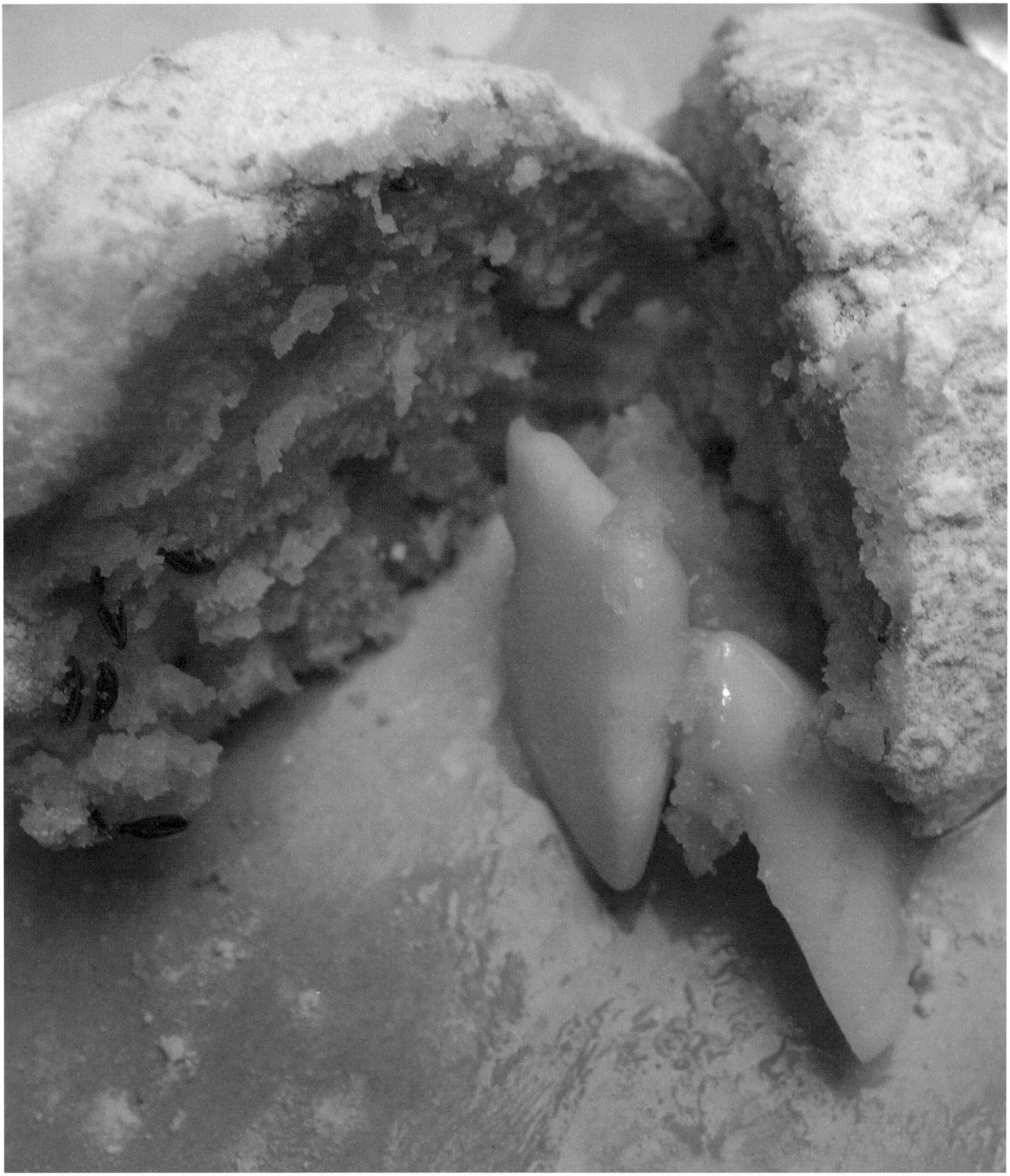

Bath Buns.

Dr. William Oliver is said to have invented these sweet buns. However, they were rich and his patients tended to put on weight, so he created his plain 'Bath Oliver' biscuits as an alternative.

William Kitchiner. 1817. 'The Cook's Oracle.'

Rub together with the hand one pound of fine flour, and half a pound of butter; beat six eggs, and add them to the flour, &c. with a table-spoonful of good yest; mix them all together, with about half a tea-cupful of milk; set it in a warm place for an hour, then mix in six ounces of sifted sugar, and a few caraway seeds; mould them into buns with a table-spoon, on a clean baking-plate; throw six or eight caraway comfits on each, and bake them in a hot oven about ten minutes.

Ingredients

(I have halved the quantities given in the original recipe. This should make 8-10 buns)

225g flour

110g butter at room temperature

1 teaspoon dried yeast

3 eggs, beaten

30ml milk at room temperature

90g icing sugar, sifted

3 teaspoons of caraway seeds

Method

1. Rub the butter into the flour then add the yeast, eggs and milk.

2. Leave for an hour in a warm place then add the icing sugar and half of the caraway seeds. Mix well.

3. Divide the mixture between bun tins lined with paper cases (the buns spread and do not retain their shape if you place them on a baking tray as in the original recipe). This makes 9-10 buns.

4. Sprinkle a little sugar and a few caraway seeds over the tops of the buns (this replaces the caraway comfits, which were candied seeds – very fiddly to make.)

5. Bake at 200°c, gas 6, for 10-15 minutes.

6. Dust them with icing sugar when they are baked.

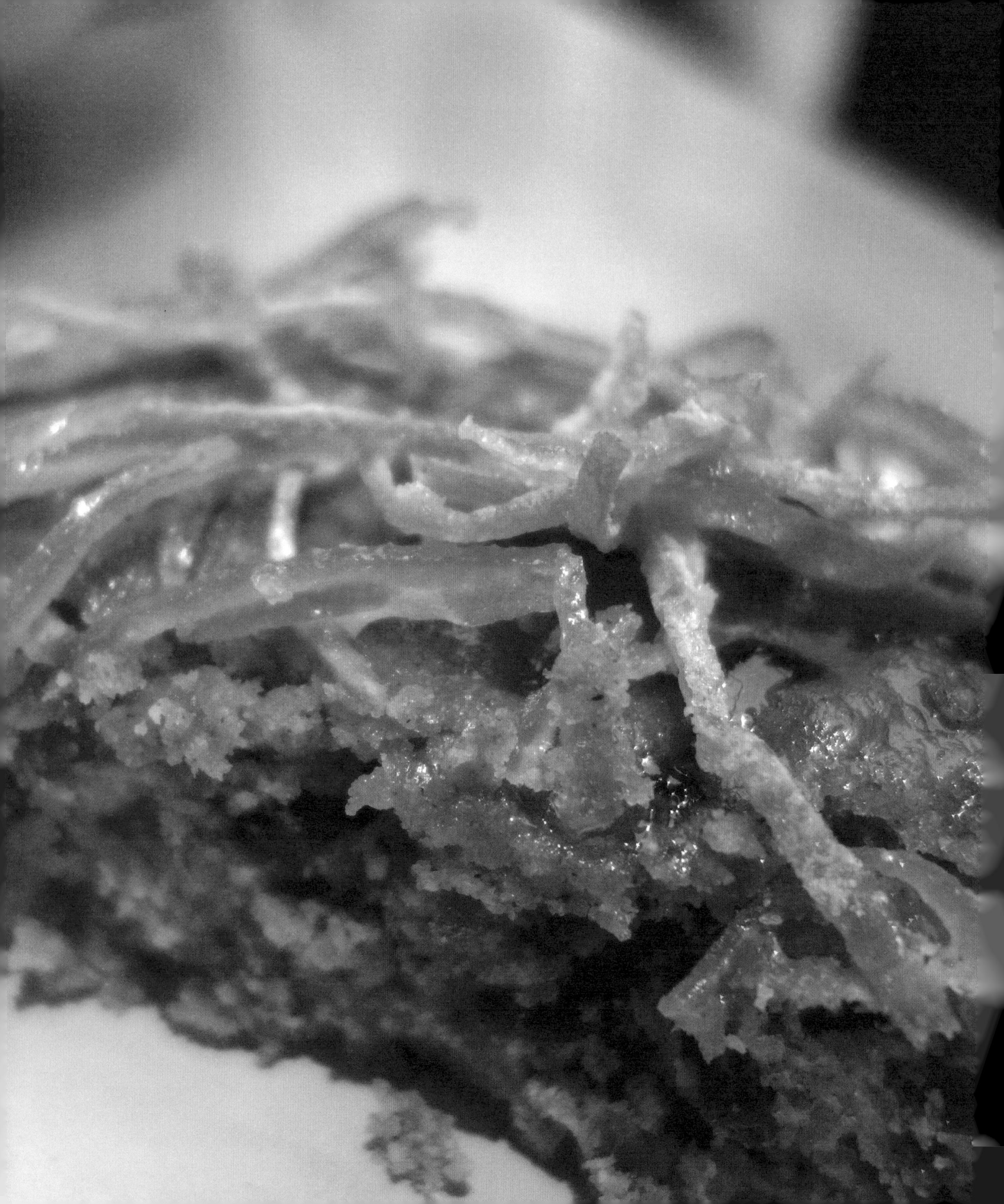

A very good Batter Cake.

Robert Smith. 1723. 'Court Cookery.'

Take six Pounds of Currans, five Pounds of Flower, an Ounce of Cloves and Mace, a little beaten Cinnamon, half an Ounce of Nutmegs, half a Pound of Sugar, three Quarters of a Pound of Citron, Lemon, and Orange-peel candied, half a Pint of Sack, a little Honey-water, a Quart of Ale-Yest, a Quart of Cream, and a Pound and three quarters of Butter melted therein; mix it well together on a Board, and lay it before the Fire to rise; then work it up, and put it in a Hoop, with a Paper flower'd at the Bottom, and so bake it. Take care not to burn it.

Ingredients

(I have divided the quantities by 10)

80g butter

270g sultanas or currants

225g self-raising flour

A pinch of ground cloves

1 teaspoon of ground mace

1 teaspoon of ground cinnamon

1 teaspoon of ground nutmeg

25g caster sugar

35g candied peel, chopped (it is good using the preserved orange from the section on 'Preserves')

30ml sherry (originally called 'sack', from the French word 'sec', or 'dry'.)

1 teaspoon of honey dissolved in 120ml warm water

1 teaspoon of dried yeast

120ml cream

Method

1. Melt the butter and allow it to cool slightly.

2. Mix all of the ingredients then leave in a warm place to rise for an hour.

3. Put the mixture into a buttered cake tin with a removable base (about 20cm).

4. Bake at 180°c, gas 4, for 25-30 minutes.

Note: this is a moist, spiced fruit cake. You can brush some melted redcurrant jelly over the top to give it a shine. Alternatively you can top the cake with some preserved orange. Or you can do both!

Chocolate Biskets.

Cocoa was originally produced in the Spanish colonies in Central America. When the British developed cocoa plantations in the West Indies it became less expensive to buy in England. It was so popular that there was a special chocolate kitchen at Hampton Court Palace, where Thomas Tosier was personal chocolate chef to both George 1st and George 2nd.

John Nott. 1723. 'The Cook and Confectioner's Dictionary.'

Scrape a little Chocolate upon the Whites of Eggs, so much as will give it the Taste and Colour of the Chocolate. Then mingle with it powder Sugar, till it becomes a pliable Paste. Then dress your Biskets upon Sheets of Paper, in what Form you please, and set them into the Oven to be bak'd with a gentle Fire, both at top and underneath.

Ingredients

3 egg whites

40g cocoa powder, sifted

100g finely grated dark chocolate

280g icing sugar, sifted

Method

1. Mix the egg whites with the cocoa and chocolate.

2. Mix in the icing sugar gently. This is a fairly soft mixture.

3. Spoon the mixture onto baking paper on a baking tray (this recipe makes about 20). Leave enough space around each for the biscuits to expand.

4. Bake for 20 minutes in the oven at 180°c, gas 4.

5. Leave to cool a little before removing the biscuits from the paper. If they don't come off easily, return the biscuits to the oven for 5-10 minutes.

Note: these are shiny, flat, dark brown chocolate meringues. This quantity makes about 20.

Chocolate Puffs.

Richard Briggs. 1788. 'The English Art of Cookery.'

Take half a pound of double-refined sugar, beat and sift it fine, scrape into it one ounce of chocolate very fine, and mix them together; beat up the white of an egg to a very high froth, then put in your chocolate and sugar, and beat it till it is as stiff as a paste; then strew sugar on some writing paper, drop them on about the size of a sixpence, and bake them in a very slow oven; when they are done take them off the paper and put them in plates.

Ingredients

1 egg white

225g icing sugar, sifted

25g chocolate, finely grated

Method

1. Whisk the egg white until stiff.

2. Add the sugar a spoonful at a time and continue to whisk.

3. Fold in the chocolate.

4. Sprinkle a couple of tablespoons of sugar onto some baking paper then drop the mixture onto it in small spoonfuls.

5. Bake in a cool oven at 140°c, gas 1-2, for 20-25 minutes.

Note: this makes 10-12 flat meringues, light brown in colour and mildly chocolaty in flavour. They are lovely with thick cream.

Gingerbread.

Ingredients

(I have used a quarter of the quantities given in the original recipe)

50g butter, at room temperature

80g caster sugar

1 egg

1 egg yolk

325g flour

225g treacle (you can replace some of this with syrup from the jar of stem ginger, if using)

2 teaspoons ground ginger

1 teaspoon caraway seeds, crushed

Half a teaspoon coriander seeds, crushed

I teaspoon grated nutmeg

100g candied peel, stem ginger in syrup, or sultanas (this is to represent the 'sweetmeats' in the original recipe)

Robert Smith. 1723. 'Court Cookery.'

Take three Pound of Flower, two pound of Treacle, two Ounces of Beaten Ginger, a few Carraway and Coriander-Seeds, eight Eggs, (the Whites but of four,), half a Pound of Butter, three Quarters of a Pound of Sugar, three Nutmegs grated, and what Sweet-meats you will: Mix these well, and Bake it in a quick Oven.

Method

1. Beat the butter and sugar together until creamy, then add the egg and egg yolk. Beat well then add the rest of the ingredients.

2. Butter a rectangular tin (28cm x 18cm) then dust it with flour.

3. Spread the mixture evenly in the tin and bake in the oven at 180°c, gas 4, for 20 minutes.

Note: this is a sweet, spicy flat bread and is good cut in slices and spread with plenty of butter.

'Sweetmeats' could be 'wet', such as preserved fruits, jellies and pastes, or 'dry', such as 'marchpane' (marzipan) and gingerbread.

To make Ginger-bread.

John Nott. 1723. 'The Cook and Confectioner's Dictionary.'

Take four Pounds of Treacle, of Citron, Lemons and Orange Peel, and candy'd Ginger, of each half a Pound; slice all these thin, add also beaten Ginger, Coriander-seeds, and Carraway-seeds, of each two Ounces; mix all these with as much Flour, as will make it a soft Paste; then lay it in Cakes on Tin-plates, and bake it in a quick Oven.

Ingredients

(I have used an eighth of the quantities given in the original recipe)

225g treacle

The zest of 2 oranges

The zest of 2 lemons

25g stem ginger, chopped

25g candied peel, chopped (or use preserved oranges. You can find the recipe in the section on 'Preserves')

1 teaspoon ground ginger

1 teaspoon ground coriander

1 teaspoon caraway seeds

225g flour

Method

1. Put the treacle, orange and lemon zest, stem ginger, candied peel, ground ginger, coriander and caraway seeds into a saucepan and heat gently for a minute until well combined.

2. Add the flour and mix to a paste.

3. Take small chunks of the paste, roll them into about 12-15 small balls and put them on baking paper on a baking tray.

4. Bake at 180°c, gas 4, for 10-12 minutes.

Note: These are intense, dark, sticky biscuits.

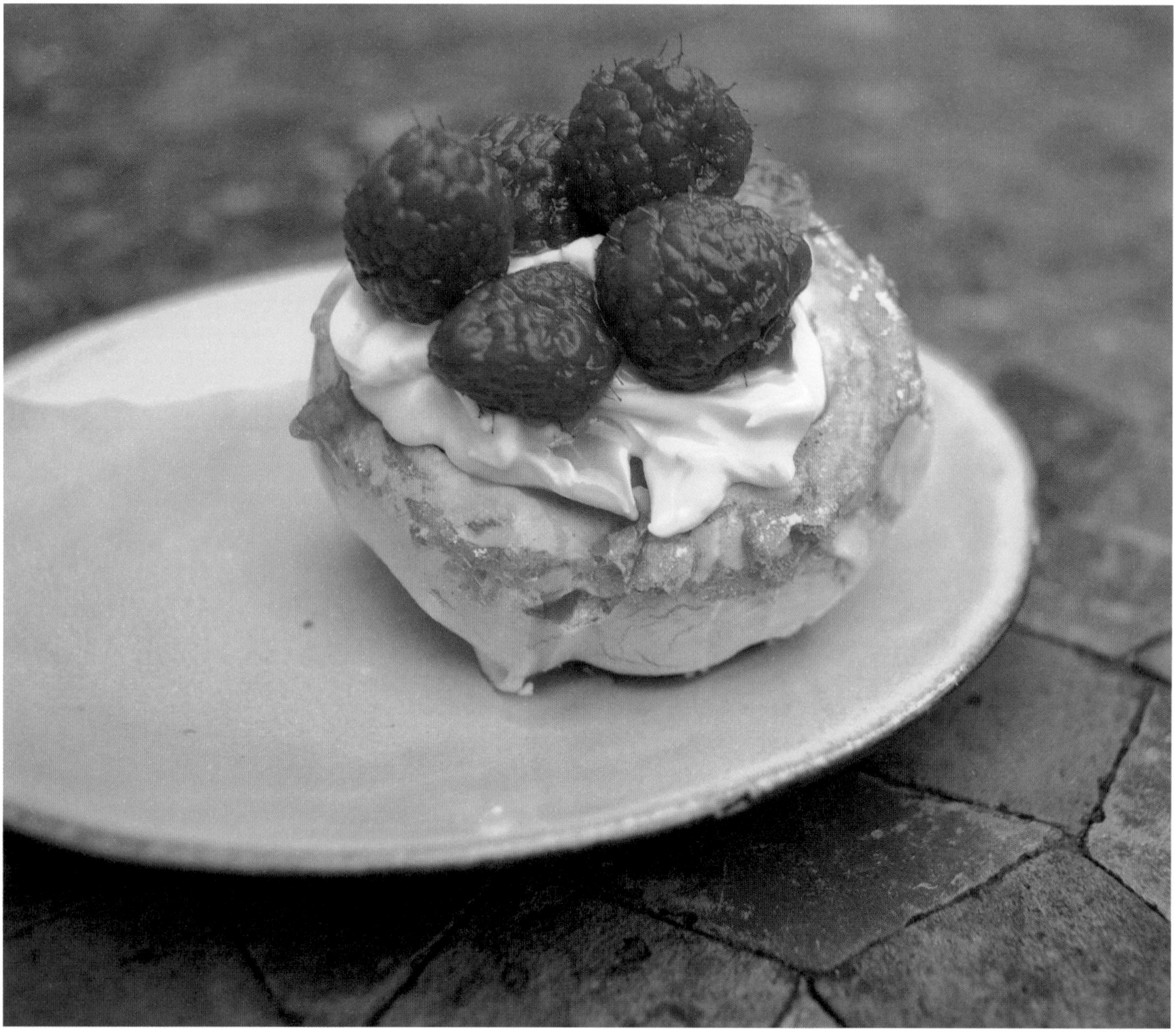

Dry Meringues.

Jarrin. 1820. 'The Italian Confectioner.'

Twelve whites of Eggs, and 1lb. Sugar

Beat up the whites of eggs; when firm, add a pound of powdered sugar, with what essence you please; lay out the paste with an iron or silver spoon into the shape of half a large egg, on sheets of paper; then cover them with sugar sifted through a silk sieve, and blow away the surplus sugar. Have a board, about two inches in thickness, on which you put the meringues to bake, as they must receive no heat but from the top; when they are of a fine colour, take them from the papers, beat in, with the back of a spoon, the liquid part to form a hollow, and then put them back into the oven to dry the inside, which is to be filled with a cream or jelly at pleasure, to be put in the moment you serve them up. Meringues are varied in taste and form, and may be ornamented with pistachios cut in fillets, and stuck in them; or currants or almonds may be added.

Ingredients

(I have halved the quantities given in the original recipe)

6 egg whites

225g icing sugar, sifted, plus a little extra

1-2 teaspoons of rose water or orange flower water

Whipped cream

Soft fruit such as strawberries or raspberries

Method

1. Whisk the egg whites until stiff then gradually whisk in the sugar. Now add the rose water or orange flower water.

2. Put spoonfuls of the mixture onto baking parchment that has been dusted with sifted icing sugar, then sift some more icing sugar over the top. The recipe tells you to blow off the excess sugar. This is messy but fun!

3. Bake on a baking tray in the oven at 100°c, gas ½, for 2 hours.

4. Turn the meringues over then, using a spoon, gently push in the base of each of them to make an indentation. Return them to the oven for another hour. Turn off the oven and leave the meringues in there until cool. They should be golden brown (not white, like modern meringues).

5. Fill the indentations with cream and fruit.

Note: This method is interesting, as a cavity is created for the cream and fruit.

You can add pistachios, currants or almonds to the mixture before cooking.

Naples Biskets.

Naples biscuits were flavoured with rose water and caraway, and used in many puddings, like the Orange Pudding in the 'Sweet Dishes' section. The correct technique involved the use of special tins to shape them, which few people owned, so many bought the biscuits from a confectioner. If you are using them for a pudding, I don't think the shape really matters, as they will be broken up or integrated into the dish.

John Nott. 1723. 'The Cook and Confectioner's Dictionary.'

Take a pound of fine flour, eight Eggs, a pound of Double refin'd loaf Sugar, and two Spoonfulls of Damask Rose-water, and an ounce of Carraway Seeds well beaten; let these be mixt well together, and made into a fit thickness with fair water, then put them into tin pans; let them be bak'd in a gentle Oven Glazing them over with Water in which Sugar has been dissolv'd.

Ingredients

(I have halved the quantities given in the original recipe)

225g flour

4 eggs

225g caster sugar

1 teaspoon of rose water

3 teaspoons caraway seeds, crushed

For the syrup: 100g sugar in 200ml water

Method

1. Mix the flour, eggs, caster sugar, rose water and caraway seeds together.

2. Butter your cake tins, preferably éclair or madeleine, to produce oblong biscuits. Dust with a little flour.

3. Divide the mixture between them and bake at 160°c, gas 3, for 15 minutes.

4. To make the syrup, place the water and sugar in a saucepan and simmer until it becomes thick and syrupy. Brush this over the cooked biscuits to give them a shine.

Note: This makes about 18 biscuits.

Ratafia Biscuits.

Jarrin suggests piping the mixture onto the baking paper, which can form a neat oblong if done correctly. You can do this if you have the equipment, but I think they look fine in this slightly rougher version. They are similar to macaroons, and were used in various puddings including Trifle and Ratafia Pudding (see the section on 'Sweet Dishes')

Ingredients

(I have divided these quantities approximately by seven)

100g almonds

1 egg white

150g icing sugar

Note: these quantities make about 12 biscuits.

Jarrin. 1820. 'The Italian Confectioner.'

1lb. bitter, ½lb. sweet Almonds; 2 lbs. Sugar, and seven whites of Eggs.

Blanch and clean the almonds, and put them in your mortar, with seven whites of eggs, and pound them very fine; then add the powdered sugar, and mix it in your mortar for a quarter of an hour, as a good ratafia biscuit cannot be made unless the sugar be well mixed in. Dress these biscuits on strong paper, or you will find it difficult to take them off; tie a pipe on the end of a bladder, but first cut a hole in the bottom of the bladder, so as just to admit the pipe, then tie it with a string; this pipe is generally about an inch and a half long; you must have it longer or smaller in the bore, according to the size of the biscuit; fill the bladder with the paste, and drop it on your paper, but the biscuits must not touch each other; bake them on plates in a warm oven; if your paper and biscuits are good, they will come off easily; but if you find them stick, wet the paper at the bottom, and they will soon come off: in this case you must put them in the stove to dry for three or four hours.

Method

1. Grind the almonds finely in a food processor.

2. Add the egg white, blend to incorporate then add most of the sugar. Blend until it comes together in a solid lump.

3. Break off small amounts and roll them into balls, using the rest of the icing sugar to stop these from sticking to the surface. Slightly flatten them then place them at intervals on baking paper on a baking tray. Alternatively you can pipe them onto the baking paper.

4. Bake at 170°c, gas 4, for 15 minutes or until set and golden. Allow them to cool completely before removing them from the paper.

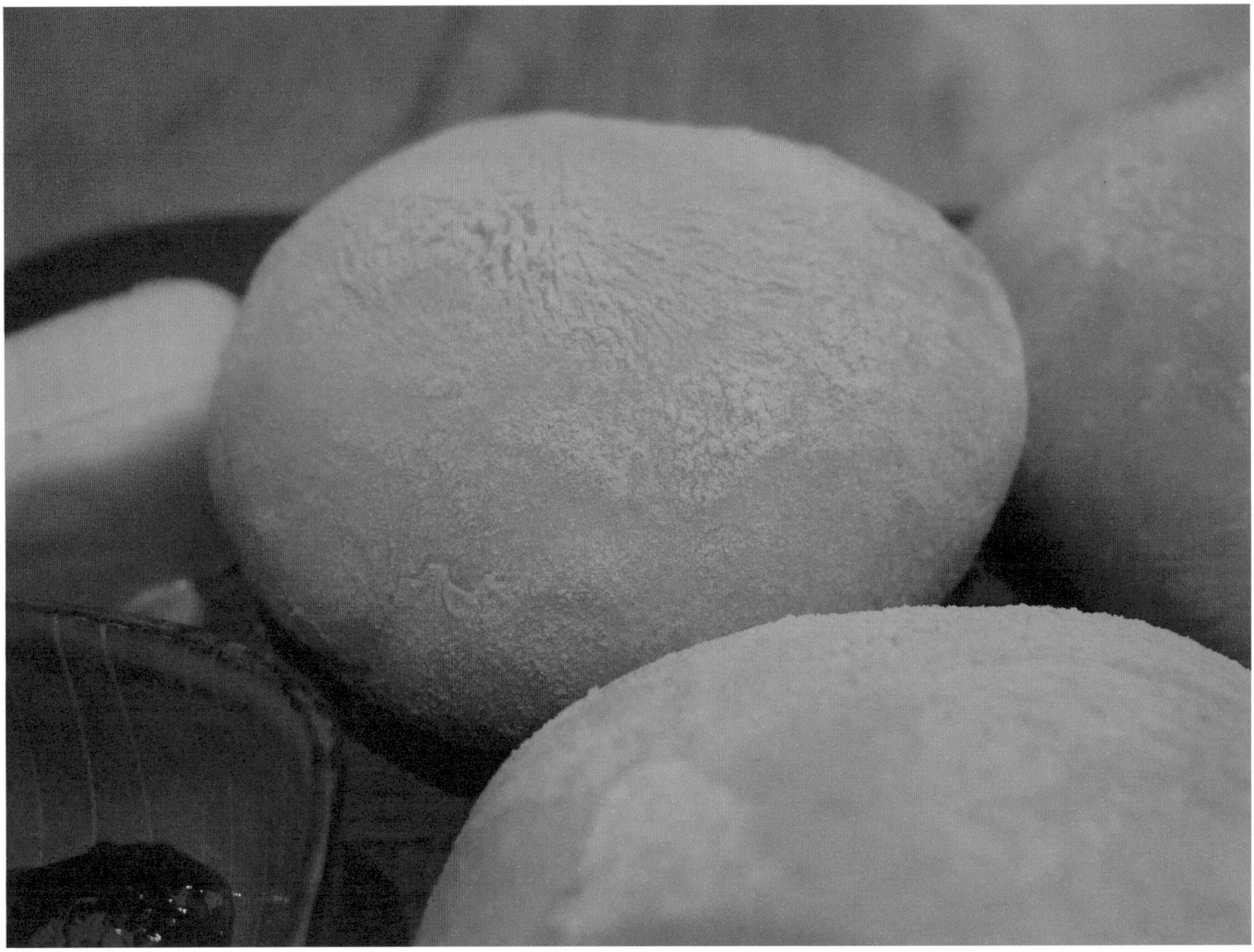

Sally Lunn Tea Cakes.

I don't know how close this recipe is to the original, which is said to be a closely guarded secret. Actually these are really just white buns, which are good toasted and served with either sweet or savoury toppings. They are named after Solange Luyon, a young Huguenot refugee from France. She arrived in Bath in 1680, bringing with her the recipe for these buns, which would have been eaten in France during festivals.

William Kitchiner. 1817. 'The Cook's Oracle.'

Take one pint of milk quite warm, a quarter of a pint of thick small-beer yest; put them into a pan with flour sufficient to make it as thick as batter, cover it over, and let it stand till it has risen as high as it will, i.e. about two hours: add two ounces of lump sugar, dissolved in a quarter of a pint of warm milk, a quarter of a pound of butter rubbed into your flour very fine; then make your dough the same as for French rolls; and let it stand half an hour; then make up your cakes, and put them on tins: when they have stood to rise, bake them in a quick oven.

Care should be taken never to put your yest to water or milk too hot, or too cold, as either extreme will destroy the fermentation. In summer it should be lukewarm, in winter a little warmer, and in very cold weather, warmer still.

When it has first risen, if you are not prepared, it will not hurt to stand an hour.

Ingredients

(I have halved the quantities given in the original recipe; this makes about 12)

350ml milk

10g dried yeast (2 teaspoons)

25g caster sugar

400g + 300g flour

50g butter, at room temperature

1 teaspoon of salt

Method

1. Warm the milk with 150ml water and add the yeast and sugar (do not overheat the liquid as this will damage the yeast)

2. Put 400g of the flour in a bowl and gradually add the milk mixture to make a batter. Cover and leave for a couple of hours, covered, in a warm place. Bubbles will start to rise to the surface.

3. Rub the butter into the remaining flour. Add the salt.

4. Add this to the batter, mix well then knead for about 5 minutes.

5. Leave this to stand in a warm place for 30 minutes.

6. Flour your work surface generously. Knead the dough gently then shape it into about 8 buns.

7. Place the buns on an ovenproof tray that has been dusted with flour. Leave them to stand until they have risen – about 30 minutes.

8. Bake in a hot oven at 200°c, gas 6, for 15-20 minutes.

Savoy Cake.

Frederick Nutt. 1809. 'The Imperial and Royal Cookbook'.

To one pound of fine sifted sugar put the yolks of ten eggs, (the whites are to be put in a separate pan); beat the yolks and sugar up well with a wooden spoon for half an hour; then whisk the whites up until they become quite stiff and white; (stir them into the batter, by little at a time); when all is in, add three quarters of a pound of flour that has been dried before the fire, and the rind of a lemon, grated; then put the mixture into the moulds; they should be baked in a very slow oven; when you think they are done, run a knife down the middle; if the knife comes out quite clean, the cakes are done; the mould should be prepared before you begin the cakes, in the following manner:-have some clarified fresh butter, and butter the moulds with a small brush, (what the painters call a tool); mix about three ounces of very fine mixed sugar with about an ounce of flour: then throw it all into one mould, and shake it about well; turn it out into the other mould, and knock the mould upon the table, so as to leave no more sugar than sticks to the mould; be very particular with the moulds: there is as much art in preparing the mould, as in the batter for the cake: when for the second course, or suppers, they are ornamented with gum paste.

Ingredients

(I have halved the quantities used in the original recipe)

5 eggs

225g icing sugar, sifted

175g plain flour and a pinch of salt

175g cornflour

The zest of a lemon, finely grated

Method

1. Whisk the egg yolks with the sugar until thick and creamy (keep the egg whites).

2. Whisk the whites until they are stiff but not dry, so that they can be folded into the egg yolks and sugar more easily.

3. Fold the egg whites into the yolks and sugar, a little at a time.

4. Sift the flour and cornflour together then add a little at a time to the mixture. Mix all together gently.

5. Butter and flour a 23cm tin with a removable base (if you want to use a smaller tin, it will produce a thicker cake, which will take a little longer to cook.) Pour in the mixture and bake in the oven at 140°c, gas 2, for an hour. Allow to cool then turn out of the tin.

Note: this is used to make trifle. It makes more than you need for the recipe in the 'Sweet Dishes' section. Cut the cake across horizontally and use a third (about 250g), or use two thirds if you are not using macaroons. You can freeze the rest, or just eat it iced or with jam and cream.

You can still buy gum paste, which is used to make decorations for cakes.

Spice Macaroons.

these are like flat, almond-flavoured meringues, with an interesting cinnamon tang. Jarrin suggests an oval shape for these cakes (as he calls them). He used spices extensively in comfits, lozenges and macaroons.

Jarrin. 1820. 'The Italian Confectioner.'

1lb. sweet Almonds; 3lbs. Sugar; eight or nine whites of Eggs; a spoonful of Cinnamon, three Cloves; and rasped Orange and Lemon Peel.

Work these ingredients as for the macaroons, with bitter almonds, except that the spices must be pounded and sifted through a silk sieve.

Ingredients

(I have used one third of the quantities given in the original recipe)

150g almonds

3 egg whites (from small eggs – about 100ml)

450g icing sugar, sifted

1 teaspoon of ground cinnamon

A pinch of ground cloves

The zest of half an orange, finely grated

The zest of half a lemon, finely grated

Method

1. Grind the almonds then blend in the egg whites.

2. Add the sugar, spices and orange and lemon zest, and blend.

3. Drop small spoonfuls of the mixture onto baking paper on a baking tray.

4. Bake in the oven at 150°c, gas 2, for 25 minutes. They should be golden brown.

Fine Spongati Italian Cake.

Ingredients

(I have used about one eighth of the quantities given in the original recipe)

Pastry:

280g flour

40g butter

35g caster sugar

1 teaspoon of olive oil

Half a teaspoon of salt

About 100ml white wine

Filling:

75g freshly made breadcrumbs, made from stale bread

70g chopped walnuts

20g currants or sultanas

20g pine nuts

275g honey

1 teaspoon of ground cinnamon

A pinch of ground cloves

1 teaspoon of ground pepper

1 teaspoon of ground nutmeg

To finish:

A little beaten egg

A little sugar

Jarrin. 1820. 'The Italian Confectioner.'

One pound six ounces of white bread, dried in the oven and reduced to a coarse powder; one pound four ounces of walnuts, blanched and chopped very fine with a double handled knife; six ounces of currants well washed and cleaned; five ounces of wild pine kernels; five pounds five ounces of virgin honey, clarified; three grains of cinnamon in powder; one grain of cloves; one grain of strong pepper; and one grain of nutmeg in powder. The above articles must be mixed together, and enclosed in a crust paste, made of the following materials, viz. two pounds eight ounces of the best wheaten floor; six ounces of fresh butter; five ounces of loaf-sugar, pounded; one ounce of olive oil of Aix in Provence, and half an ounce of salt, with a sufficient quantity of white wine to mix the whole. This paste being of a moderate consistence, is to be formed into round cases or crusts, into which the first mixture is to be introduced, and a cover of the same paste must be put on, which must be pricked all over with the point of the knife. Let them stand for a whole day, put them in an oven, moderately heated, on plates dusted over with flour; these cakes should be an inch thick: they may be iced or not, as you please.

Method

1. First make the pastry. Rub the butter into the flour then add the sugar, oil and salt, with enough white wine to bind it into a paste. Roll out the pastry thinly then cut out circles and put them into small tart tins, which have been buttered and dusted with flour.

2. Combine all of the ingredients for the filling. Put some into each of the tart cases then cover each with a circle of pastry and prick with the tip of a sharp knife. Leave them to stand for at least a couple of hours.

3. Brush the tops with beaten egg, sprinkle with sugar then bake at 180°c, gas 4 for 15 minutes. Lift them out of the tins and place on a baking tray. Brush the sides with egg and return to the oven for 10 minutes.

Note: this makes about 10-12 individual tarts. You can also make a larger version in a cake tin with a removable base. This takes longer to cook.

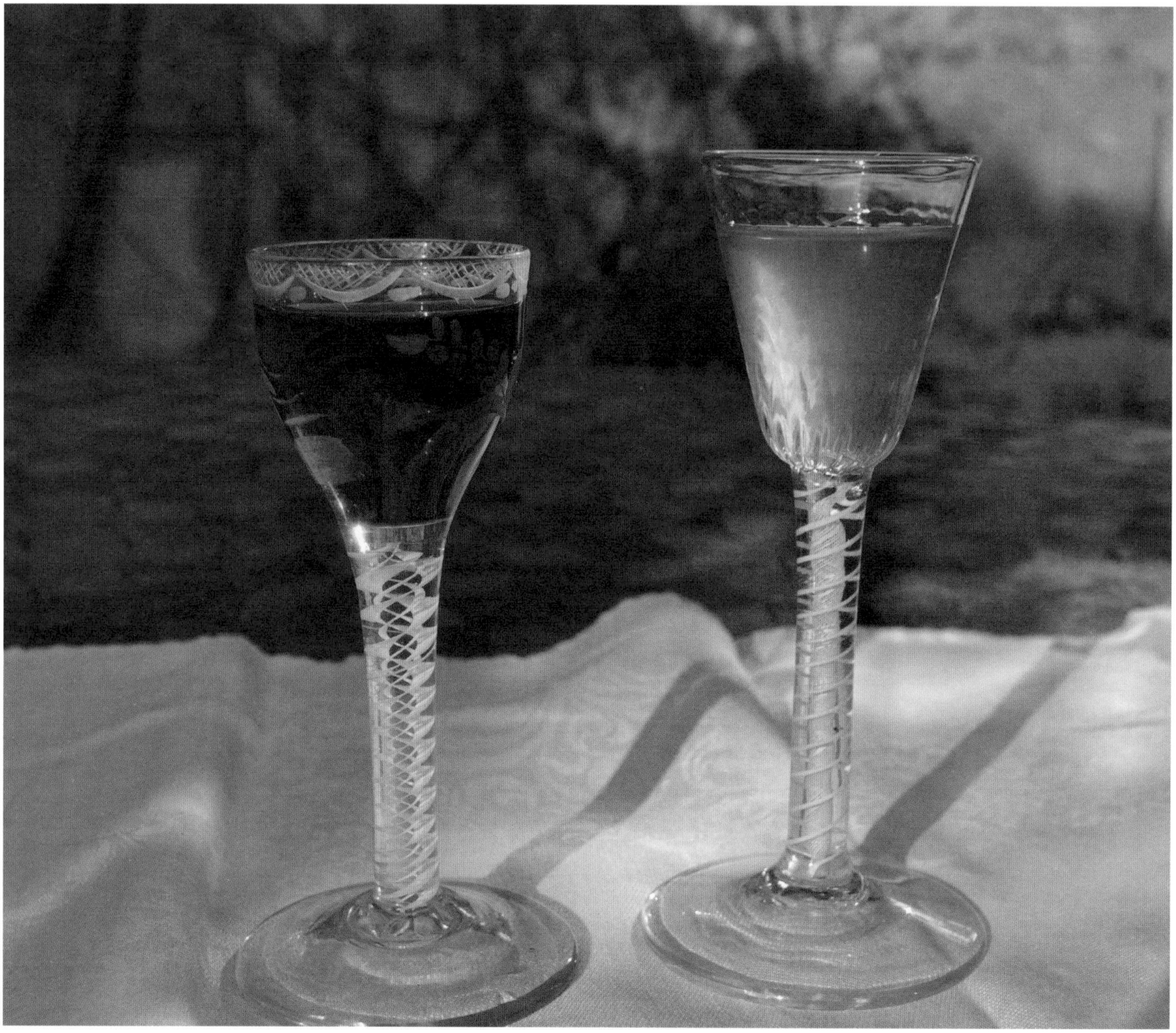

Cordial glasses on loan from Old Bank Antiques, London Road, Bath

Drinks

' Mr. Banister having lately taken from the smugglers a freight of brandy,
entertained Mr. Carman, Mr. Fuller, and myself, in the even, with a bowl of punch.'

Thomas Turner. 'Diary of a Georgian Shopkeeper. 1754 – 1765

The Georgians consumed a great deal of alcohol. Beer was seen as a healthy drink, especially among the poor, and was less impure than water. It varied greatly in strength and quality, from a sparkling ale that was served in champagne-style flutes to 'small beer', which had a low alcohol content and so was considered suitable for servants and even children.

Taverns and inns were popular among those who travelled by coach. However, the drinks they served were far from reliable in terms of quality. Tom Jones *'called for a Pint of Wine to be mulled. She immediately obeyed, by putting the same Quantity of Perry to the Fire: For this readily answered to the Name of every Kind of Wine.'* (1746. Henry Fielding.)

Some excellent, if expensive, wines were imported from Europe, and James Boswell referred to the beneficial qualities of a rich Languedoc wine: *'it will comfort you, as it has done me, often and often, for it is not such wine as one gets every day'.* (1791. 'The Life of Samuel Johnson.')

Wine was thought to be beneficial to people's health. In Northanger Abbey, John Thorpe claims that *'if every body was to drink their bottle a-day, there would not be half the disorders in the world there are now.... There is not the hundredth part of the wine consumed in this kingdom that there ought to be. Our foggy climate wants help.'* (1818. Jane Austen)

However, Samuel Richardson's heroine, Clarissa,

warns against the dangers to women of drinking wine: *'How many women have been taken advantage by wine, and other still more intoxicating viands?'* (1748)

The diarist Parson Woodford admitted to drinking wine with his breakfast on a Sunday morning: *'Before we went to Church there was Chocolate and Toast and Cake with red Wine and White.'* (1985. 'A Country Parson: James Woodforde's Diary 1759-1802.') It would be interesting to know how this impacted on his sermons.

There were vineyards in England, and the cookery writer Richard Bradley described how to make the wines *'stronger and richer than they have usually been'.* (1727. 'The Country Housewife and Lady's Director.')

Not everyone appreciated these local wines. Tobias Smollett wrote: *' there is no nation that drinks so hoggishly as the English. What passes for wine among us, is not the juice of the grape. It is an adulterous mixture, brewed up of nauseous ingredients, by dunces, who are bunglers in the art of poison-making; and yet we, and our forefathers, are and have been poisoned by this cursed drench, without taste or flavour'.* (1771. 'Humphrey Clinker'.)

In the homes of the affluent, wine was served cold, the bottles being kept in large wine coolers, filled with ice. Daniel Defoe's heroine, Roxana, described *'a great Cistern for Bottles, which cost a hundred and twenty Pound'.* (1724)

After dinner the men often drank port, which was believed to be a healthy drink. The diarist Parson Woodforde was recommended by his doctor to drink more to help with his *'uncommon sinkings': 'I drank plentifully of Port Wine after dinner, instead of one Glass, drank 7 or 8 Wine Glasses, and it seemed to do me much good, being better for it.'* Unsurprisingly this episode was followed by an attack of gout.

Rum was popular as a drink for sailors, served with lemon juice to combat scurvy. This habit spread and Thomas Turner, author of the 'Diary of a Georgian Shopkeeper 1754-1765', was fond of a drink called 'Bumboo', which was made of rum, water, sugar and nutmeg or cinnamon. (1979)

Rum was made from molasses, a by-product of the sugar-making process, produced by enslaved people on West Indian Plantations, and so some people refused to drink it on principle.

An advertisement for rum from the Bath chronicle in 1761 shows that *'Very large Quantities of Jamaica rum'* were sold in Ludgate Hill in London. It was *'delivered from on board the Ships now in the River at 4s. 6d. per Gallon.'*

William 3rd of Holland introduced gin to England, as an alternative to brandy from France. Not only did this overcome the problems of supply resulting from the difficult relations with France, with whom

England was often at war, but it was also a way of using up the corn surplus. It was called 'Dutch Geneva', referring to the juniper berries with which it was made. Gin was easy to produce and it was soon cheaper than beer or porter.

Parson Woodforde, clearly unaware of the dangers of drinking gin, described how a *'poor Woman from Dereham with a small Child with her was taken very ill with a violent pain within her by my great Gates and was laid down in the road. I went out to her and gave her a good Glass of Gin and gave her sixpence to go to the Inn...'* (1985. 'A Country Parson: James Woodforde's Diary 1759-1802.')

He also gave a *'glass of Geneva'* to *'Andrews the Smuggler'*, with whom he was clearly on very friendly terms. (1985. 'A Country Parson: James Woodforde's Diary 1759-1802.')

'Cordials', in addition to being a useful method of preserving fruit in alcohol, were used to treat a range of ailments. In novels of the time, heroines were frequently given cordials to revive their spirits, as in 'Persuasion' when Louisa had her accident. (1818. Jane Austen). The alcoholic content would explain the popularity of this remedy.

Spices, believed to have health-giving properties, were sometimes added to them. Henry Howard, the London cook, suggested cumin, added to wine, as a cure for 'stinking breath'. (1703 'England's Newest Way in Cookery'.) It seems unlikely that this would have improved matters.

Cool Drinks for Balls.

Raspberry water.

Jarrin. 1820. 'The Italian Confectioner.'

Currant, Cherry, Strawberry, and Raspberry Waters, are in general made by mashing either of the above fruits, straining the juice through a sieve, and afterwards through a flannel bag; water is then added, with syrup, to the taste; strain it again through the bag, ice it, and serve it up very fresh. But the liquor is never so transparent or clear as when the fruit is boiled in the water.

Ingredients

100g sugar

300ml water

300g raspberries

Method

1. Put the sugar and water in a large saucepan and heat gently to dissolve the sugar.

2. Add the raspberries and boil for 10 minutes to make a syrup.

3. Pass the raspberry syrup through a fine sieve into a jug.

4. Pour the syrup into a bottle and allow to cool.

5. Chill in the fridge and serve with ice.

Note: this is a refreshing drink, and would have been ideal for revitalising the young women who were dancing at a ball. I tried making the syrup and mixing this with the raspberries, without boiling them. As described in the recipe above, the colour of the 'water' was not as good.

Lemonade.

This recipe is also in the section on 'Cool Drinks for Balls, Routes, &c.' in Jarrin's book.

In Croome Park there is a very grand 'temple greenhouse', Robert Adam's first garden building. It was similar to an orangery and would have housed lemons and other citrus plants, as well as displaying 'tender exotics' from the earl's collection. It had under-floor heating fed by a furnace in the brick bothy (a shed or basic accommodation for gardeners)

Jarrin. 1820. 'The Italian Confectioner.'

Take the outside of the rinds of six lemons, cut as fine as possible, and put them into two quarts of water; then cut your lemons in halves, squeeze the juice into the water, and add syrup to your taste; mix the ingredients well, and let them stand for some time ; strain the liquor through a flannel bag, and ice it.

Ingredients

(I have halved the quantities used in the original recipe)

300g sugar

300ml water

3 lemons

Method

1. Dissolve the sugar in the water and boil for 3 minutes (this makes a syrup)

2. Add the zest of the lemons and boil for another 3 minutes.

3. Add the juice of the lemons and leave for at least an hour for the flavours to infuse.

4. Strain into a bottle and keep in the fridge until required.

5. Dilute to taste and serve with ice.

Lemonade in a Minute.

William Kitchiner. 1817. 'The Cook's Oracle.'

Pound a quarter of an ounce of citric acid, with a few drops of quintessence of lemon-peel, and mix it by degrees with a pint of clarified syrup or syrup of lemons. The proportion of acid to the syrup, was that selected (from several specimens) by the committee of taste. We advise those who are disposed to verify our receipt, to mix only three quarters of a pint of syrup first, and add the other quarter if they find it too acid. If you have no quintessence of lemon-peel, flavour your syrup with thin-cut lemon-peel, or use syrup of lemon-peel. A table-spoonful of this in a pint of water will immediately produce a very agreeable sherbet; the addition of rum or brandy will convert this into Punch.

Ingredients

2 teaspoons citric acid

1 teaspoon of 'quintessence' or tincture of lemon-peel (this is made by putting lemon zest in a jar of brandy and leaving it for two weeks.)

600ml syrup of lemons (this is made by warming 300ml lemon juice with 400g sugar and the thinly sliced zest of a lemon. Simmer for a few minutes then strain into a bottle.)

Method

1. Mix the citric acid with the 'quintessence' or tincture of lemons then add the syrup of lemons

2. Dilute this according to taste (Kitchiner suggests a tablespoon to a pint of water) and add it to rum or brandy to make punch.

Note: this recipe is relatively quick to make, but first you have to make your essence of lemon and your syrup! In fact the tincture of lemon peel is a very useful way of using lemon zest from unwaxed lemons, when you are only using the juice. All you do is soak it in brandy for a couple of weeks, and *'it will impregnate the spirit with the flavour very strongly.'*

Kitchiner's recipe for lemonade was useful for making various versions of punch:

'Brandy or rum, flavoured with lemonade, will give you very good extempore "essence of punch." The addition of a quart of Sherry or Madeira makes "punch royal;" if, instead of wine, the above quantity of water be added, it will make "punch for chambermaids.'

Punch-Royal.

Note: at balls it was seen as crucial to provide plenty of alcohol to create a relaxed atmosphere. Punch was a popular drink, made with brandy or rum, mixed with water or milk, lime or lemon juice, and spices. It was ladled from a large bowl into glasses called rummers, and served as a stimulant to encourage dancing.

At Erdigg in Wales, the marble wine cistern was filled with 20 gallons of punch for Simon Yorke's coming-of-age party in 1792.

John Nott. 1723. 'The Cook and Confectioner's Dictionary.'

Take three pints of the best brandy, as much spring-water, a pint or better of the best lime-juice, a pound of double refined sugar. This punch is better than weaker punch, for it does not so easily affect the head, by reason of the large quantity of lime-juice more than common, and is more grateful and comfortable to the stomach.

Ingredients

(I have used a quarter of the quantities given in the original recipe)

450ml brandy

450ml water

150ml lime juice – about 4 limes

100g caster sugar

Method

1. Mix the brandy with the water, lime juice and sugar.

2. Pour this into bottles, stopper them and store in a cool place.

Punch for Chamber-maids.

At Ickworth in Suffolk, they held balls for the servants in the library. There is a rosewood piano, which may well have been played to encourage dancing.

Servants were often given alcoholic drinks, especially beer, as part of their wages, as it was believed that it would make them work harder.

John Nott. 1723. 'The Cook and Confectioner's Dictionary.'

Take a Quart of Water, a quarter of a Pint of Lime-juice; squeeze in also the Juice of a Sevil Orange and a Lemon; put in six ounces of fine Sugar; strain all through a Strainer, three times till it is very clear; then put in a Pint of Brandy, and half a Pint of White-wine._

Ingredients

(I have halved the quantities used in the original recipe)

600ml water

75ml lime juice – 2-3 limes

Juice of half an orange

Juice of half a lemon

85g caster sugar

300ml brandy

150ml white wine

Method

1. Mix the water, lime juice, orange juice, lemon juice and sugar and pass the liquid through a fine sieve three times.

2. Add the brandy and wine.

3. Pour this into bottles, stopper them and store in a cool place.

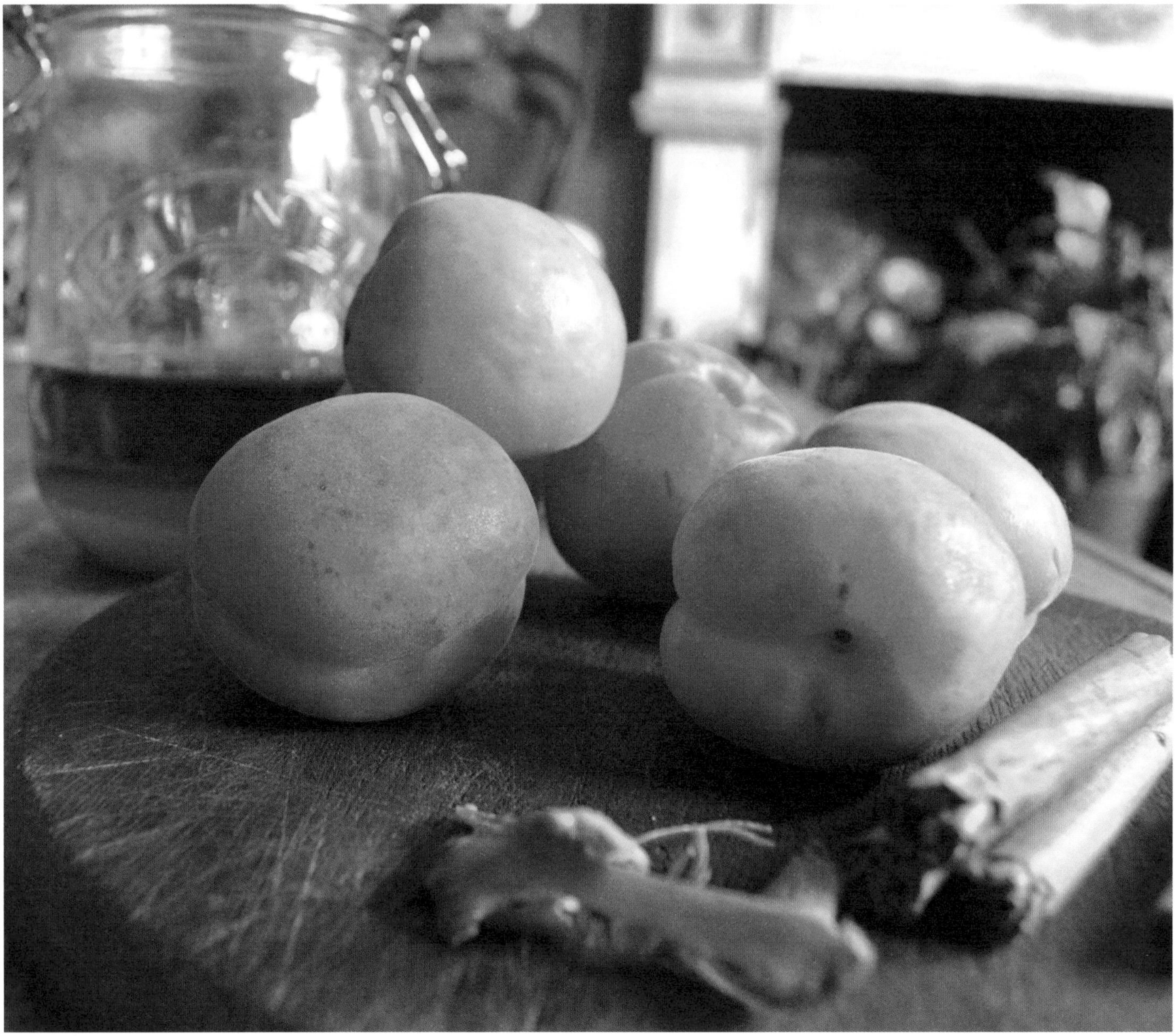

Ratafia of Apricots.

Apricot kernels were often added to give the drink a nutty flavour, but if too many are consumed they can have a toxic effect (they contain cyanide!). However, some believe that in moderation they can be effective in the prevention of cancer.

Ratafia can also refer to a kind of almond biscuit that is similar to a macaroon.

John Nott. 1723. 'The Cook and Confectioner's Dictionary.'

You may either cut the Apricocks in pieces, and infuse them in Brandy for a Day or two, and pass them through a straining Bag, and put in the usual Ingredients: Or else you may boil the Apricocks in White-wine, and put the Brandy to them; allowing a quarter of a Pound of Sugar to every Quart, with the Kernels of the Apricocks, Mace, Cloves, and Cinnamon: Let these infuse for eight or ten Days, then strain it, and bottle it up for use.

Ingredients

500g apricots, halved or quartered according to size

600ml brandy

55g sugar

1 blade of mace

2 cloves

1 stick of cinnamon

Method

1. Crack a few of the apricot stones to extract the kernels and slice them. Put the kernels and the apricots into a kilner jar with the brandy, sugar, mace, cloves and cinnamon and shake well.

2. Shake daily for 8-10 days

3. Strain the liquid and pour into a bottle to store.

Note: ratafia was a popular fruit cordial. I prefer to use less brandy (500ml) and more sugar (100 – 150g) than the original recipe as I like it to be sweet, but you can experiment with the quantities to make a personalised version. The original recipe also suggests cooking the apricots in wine (I used 300ml). This is good too. After straining off the apricots, they can be cooked with sugar to make a compote, which has a lovely brandy flavour.

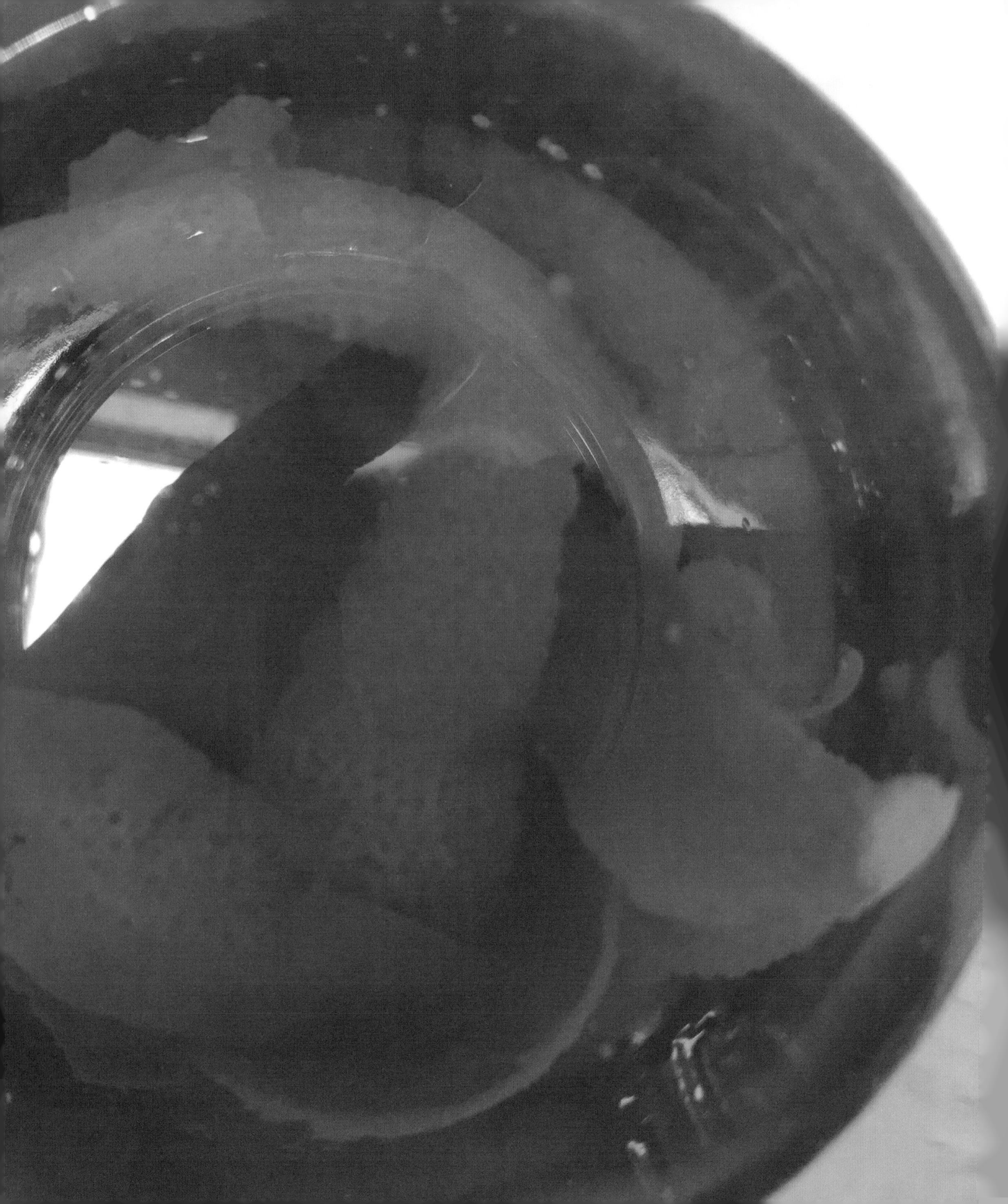

Ratafia of Orange.

Jarrin wrote that: 'Every liqueur made by infusions, is called ratafia; that is, when the spirit is made to imbibe thoroughly the aromatic flavour and colour of the fruit steeped in it: when this has taken place, the liqueur is drawn off, and sugar added to it; it is then filtered and bottled.'

Orange trees were planted in large pots in orangeries, where they were protected from the frost in winter. They could be moved outside in the summer, and were seen as an exotic addition to the gardens of the wealthy.

In 'The Mysteries of Udolpho', Ann Radcliffe described an idyllic garden containing orange trees: 'in the centre a fountain continually refreshed the air, and seemed to heighten the fragrance, that breathed from the surrounding orangeries'. (1794). Jane Austen mocked the gothic style of this book in 'Northanger Abbey', written in the same year.

Jarrin. 1820. 'The Italian Confectioner.'

Six China oranges, two pounds of sugar, four pints of brandy, and one pint of water.

Peel six fine oranges, infuse the rind in the brandy for fifteen day; melt your sugar in the cold water, and strain - And filter the liqueur and bottle it.

Ingredients

(I have divided the quantities in the original recipe by 6)

1 mandarin orange or tangerine

400ml brandy

100ml water

150g sugar

Method

1. Cut the zest of the mandarin orange into strips, put these into a large jar and pour over the brandy. Cover and leave for 15 days

2. Pour the water into a saucepan and add the sugar. Heat gently to dissolve the sugar (this works better than using cold water as suggested in the original recipe)

3. Pour the sugar and water over the orange zest and brandy then strain into a bottle. Jarrin doesn't specify how long you have to leave it before drinking. It tastes good immediately!

Ratafia of Raspberries.

Advertisements for brandy could be found in newspapers, such as this one from the Bath Chronicle, January 1761: *'At the Vaults, Cellars, and Ware-Houses, under and adjoining to his House On LUDGATE HILL, LONDON, CONIAC BRANDY. The oldest and best that can possibly be imported, at 9s. 6d. Per Gallon.'*

Smugglers brought a great deal of brandy into England, most of which came from France. Few challenged this practice, and it was common to serve 'nantzy' or French brandy from Nantes, without any questions being asked.

Parson Woodforde had a regular supplier, who delivered it to the door: *'We heard a thump at the Front Door about that time, but did not know what it was, till I went out and found the 2 Tubs – but nobody there.'* ('A Country Parson: James Woodforde's Diary, 1759-1802.')

Jarrin. 1820. 'The Italian Confectioner.'

Raspberries ten pounds, sugar four pounds, brandy ten pints, cinnamon two drachms, cloves one drachm.

Infuse the articles for fifteen days, stir the mixture every day, strain it through a bag, and filter it.

Ingredients

(I have divided the quantities in the original recipe by 20)

225g raspberries

90g sugar

300ml brandy

1 cinnamon stick

4 cloves

Method

1. Combine all of the ingredients in a large jar and leave for 15 days, stirring daily.

2. Strain this through a muslin bag or fine sieve and bottle it.

Note: Once you have strained off the raspberries, they are very good eaten with cream or yoghurt.

Scrub.

Sarah Harrison. 1733. 'The House-Keeper's Pocket-Book.'

To nine Quarts of Brandy put two Quarts of Lemon-juice, and four Pounds of Loaf Sugar; infuse Half of the Lemon-peels in the Brandy twenty four Hours, then put it into a Cask that holds near, or exact the Quantity; let it be well rolled and jumbled once a Day, for four or five Days; let it stand till it is fine, and then bottle it off. A few Oranges do well amongst the Lemons. If it be made of Orange-juice, half the Quantity of Sugar will do; but if it be half Lemons, and half Oranges, three Pounds of Sugar will not be sufficient, which I have found by Experience.

N.B. The above Receipt is right, if you would make it rich and good; if you would make it poorer, then you may put in more Brandy. It generally fines in ten or twelve Days, but it should not be bottled off till it is perfectly fine.

Ingredients

(I have divided the quantities in the original recipe by 16)

4 lemons

675ml brandy

Juice of an orange

110g sugar

Method

1. Soak the zest of 2 lemons in the brandy for 24 hours in a large kilner jar with a seal.

2. Add the rest of the lemon zest and the lemon and orange juice.

3. Add the sugar and shake the jar once a day for 4-5 days.

4. Leave to stand until the mixture becomes clear (about 10-12 days) then strain into a bottle.

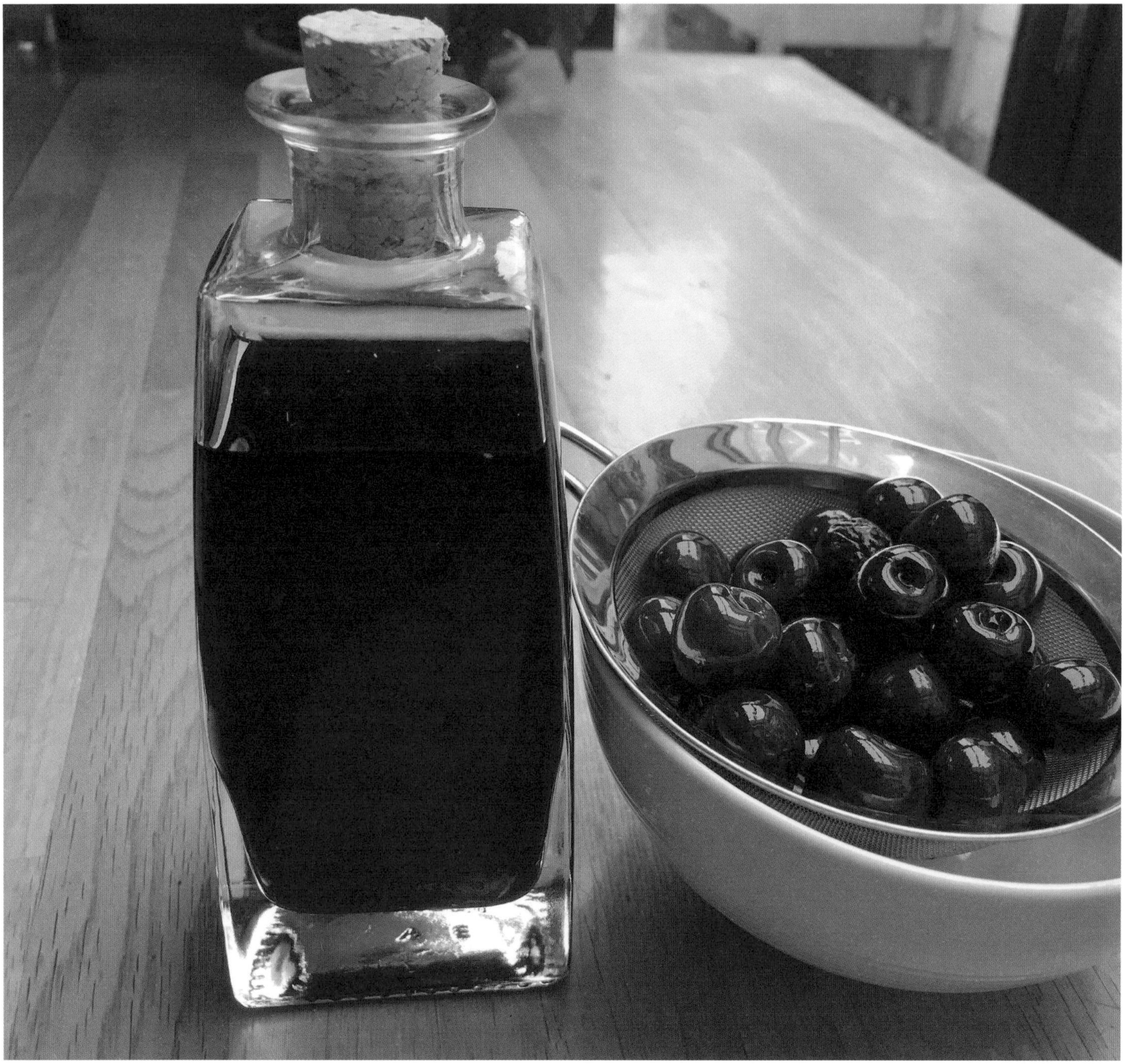

Visney.

This is a cherry liqueur, or 'cordial' as the Georgians would have called it. The inspiration is probably from Eastern Europe. There is a Romanian sour cherry brandy called visinata, and a Polish cherry brandy called wisniak.

Richard Bradley. 1730. 'The Country Housewife.'

This Visney is made of pure Brandy, and as many Morello Cherries as will fill the Bottles or Casks, with one Ounce of Loaf-Sugar to each full Quart; these Vessels or Bottles muſt be gently stopp'd, when the Cherries are put in, and stand in a cool Cellar for two Months before the Liquor is poured from them, and then the Liquor may be put in small Bottles for use: It is not very strong, but very pleasant. The Cherries, when they are taken out, may be distill'd, and will yield a fine Spirit.

Ingredients

(I have used a quarter of the quantities used in the original recipe)

225g morello cherries, stalks removed

50g sugar (I have added more sugar, as I like the drink to be a little sweeter than in the original recipe)

200ml brandy

Method

1. Put the cherries into a large jar and add the sugar and brandy. Cover or seal the jar.

2. Leave for two months in a cool place

3. Strain the liquid into a bottle.

Note: After straining off the cherries, I cook them in a little sugar or honey to make a compote. They retain the brandy flavour, which is very good.

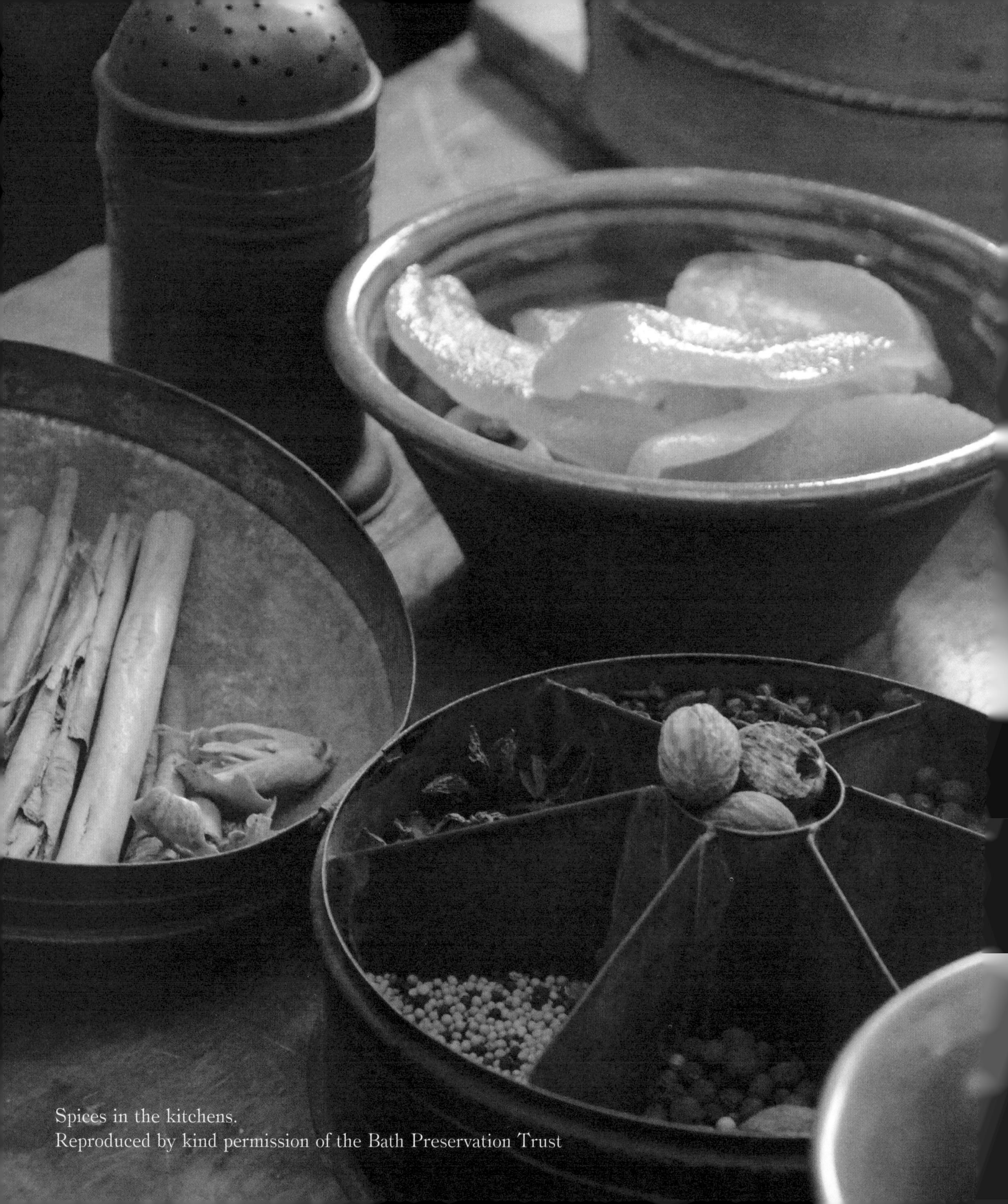

Spices in the kitchens.
Reproduced by kind permission of the Bath Preservation Trust

Preserves

*'I advise you to lay in a Store of Spices, bought at some noted reputable
Grocer's, as Nutmeg, Cloves, Mace, Cinnamon, Ginger, Jamaica Pepper,
Black Pepper, and Long Pepper, that you may have every one ready at Hand'.*

Sarah Harrison. 1773. 'The House Keeper's Pocket Book.'

The efficient storage and preservation of food was essential to ensure there would be enough to last through the winter.

In large houses much of the preservation of fruit would have been carried out in the 'still room', overseen by the housekeeper. *'All sorts of fruits are prepared as if to be preserved, except that they are not boiled so much: in winter you must use preserves, which must be taken from their own syrup to be put into a thinner one, with the juice of a lemon.'* (1820. Jarrin. 'The Italian Confectioner.')

In more ordinary households, fruit grown in orchards and walled gardens could be made into jams to provide an important source of vitamins over the winter. The diarist Parson Woodforde described his niece making jam: *'Nancy very busy this morning in making some Rasberry Jam and red Currant jelly. She made to day about 8 Pd. Of Currant jelly and about 9 Pound of Rasberry Jam.'* (1985. 'A Country Parson: James Woodforde's Diary, 1759-1802.')

Breakfast was often a social occasion, with cold meats, cake and bread with jams and marmalade. Samuel Johnson enjoyed a gloriously excessive breakfast in 1776 with his friend Margaret Dodds, who served seven types of bread and a choice of raspberry, cherry or apple jam, as well as marmalade.

Jane Austen used food or meals to show a person's position in society. In 'Northanger Abbey', the superiority of the Tilney family could be seen in the quality of the breakfast served. Catherine admired the *'elegance of the breakfast set'*, and went on to say that *'never in her life before had she beheld half such variety on a breakfast-table'.* (1818)

Public breakfasts were fashionable at pleasure gardens such as in the spa town of Bath, at the Sydney Hotel (now the Holburne Museum), where the dining boxes were arranged in two curves, overlooking the gardens. There was a charge of 6d for the waiter to bring a teapot containing tea-leaves, and a kettle of boiling water, so that the tea was freshly made even if you were in a part of the grounds that was far away from the house.

The other famous pleasure gardens of Bath were the Spring Gardens, opposite the Orange Grove. Fashionable people went in their sedan chairs, which were carried across the river on a ferryboat. There were public breakfasts with music on Mondays and Thursdays. On other days there was no music and so the breakfast cost less. In 'Humphrey Clinker', a letter from Lydia Melford in Bath described Bath's Spring-garden as: *'a sweet retreat, laid out in walks and ponds, and parterres of flowers; and there is a long-room for breakfasting and dancing.'* (1771. 'Tobias Smollett)

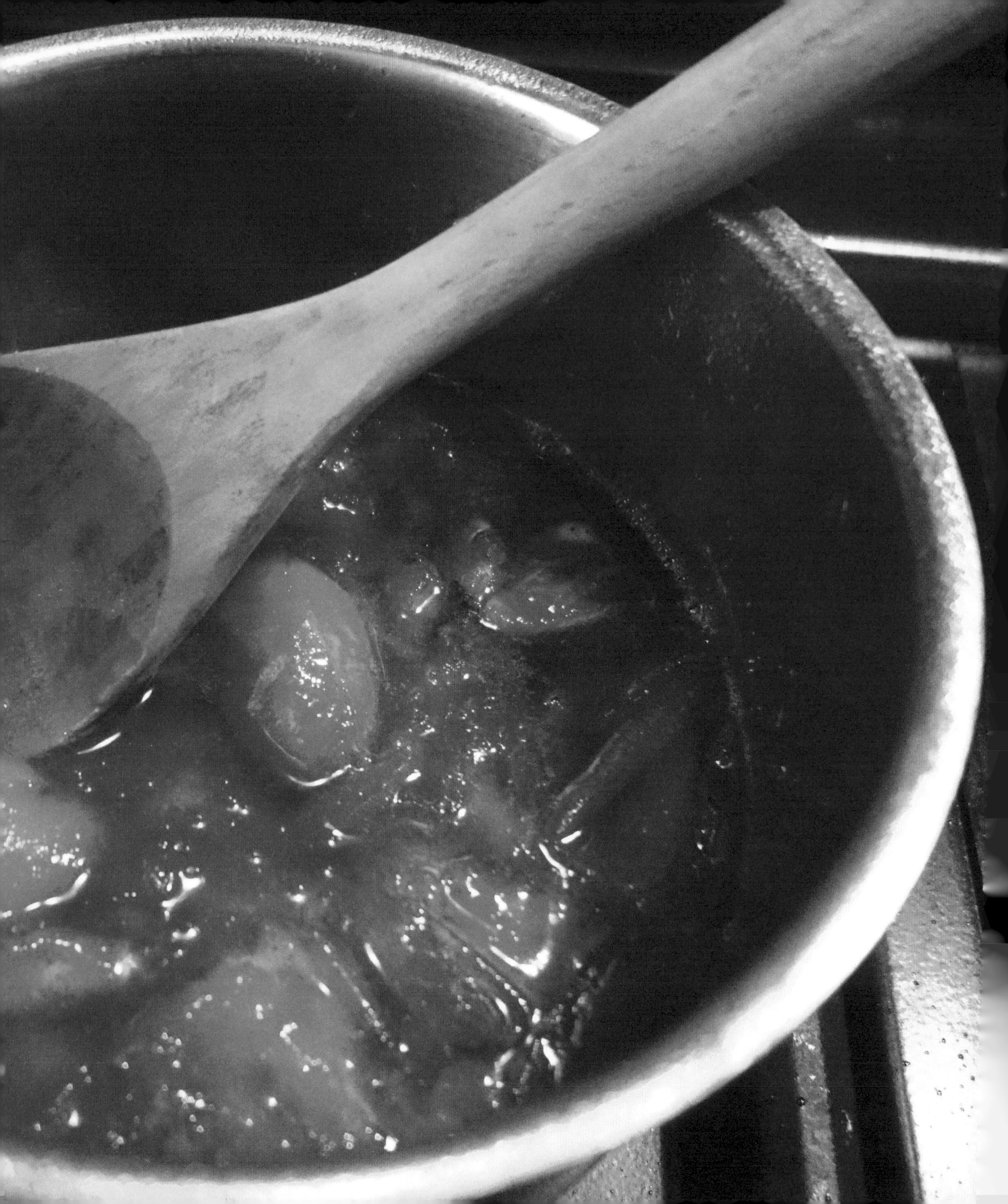

Apricot, or any Plum Jam.

William Kitchiner. 1817. 'The Cook's Oracle and Housekeeper's Manual.'

After taking away the stones from the apricots, and cutting out any blemishes they may have, put them over a slow fire, in a clean stew-pan, with half a pint of water; when scalded, rub them through a hair-sieve: to every pound of pulp put one pound of sifted loaf-sugar; put it into a preserving-pan over a brisk fire, and when it boils skim it well, and throw in the kernels of the apricots, and half an ounce of bitter almonds, blanched; boil it a quarter of an hour fast, and stirring it all the time; remove it from the fire, and fill it into pots, and cover them.

N.B. Green gages or plums may be done in the same way, omitting the kernels or almonds.

Ingredients

(I have halved the quantities used in the original recipe)

400g apricots or plums

150ml water

About 300g caster sugar

10g almonds, flaked or cut into slivers

Method

1. Quarter the apricots or plums then remove the stones, cracking them open to obtain the kernels (if you cut the kernels in half, you can peel their skin off fairly easily).

2. Put the apricots or plums and water into a pan and boil for 20 minutes, until the fruit is soft.

3. Push the fruit and liquid through a sieve into a bowl.

4. Weigh the fruit pulp and put it into a clean pan with an equal amount of sugar and bring to the boil. Simmer for 15 minutes, stirring to make sure it doesn't stick to the bottom of the pan. Skim off any foam.

5. Add the almonds and apricot or plum kernels.

6. Simmer for 15 minutes then put the jam into jars and cover tightly. Store in a cool place.

Note: apricot kernels were added to give the jam a nutty flavour, but if too many are consumed they can have a toxic effect.

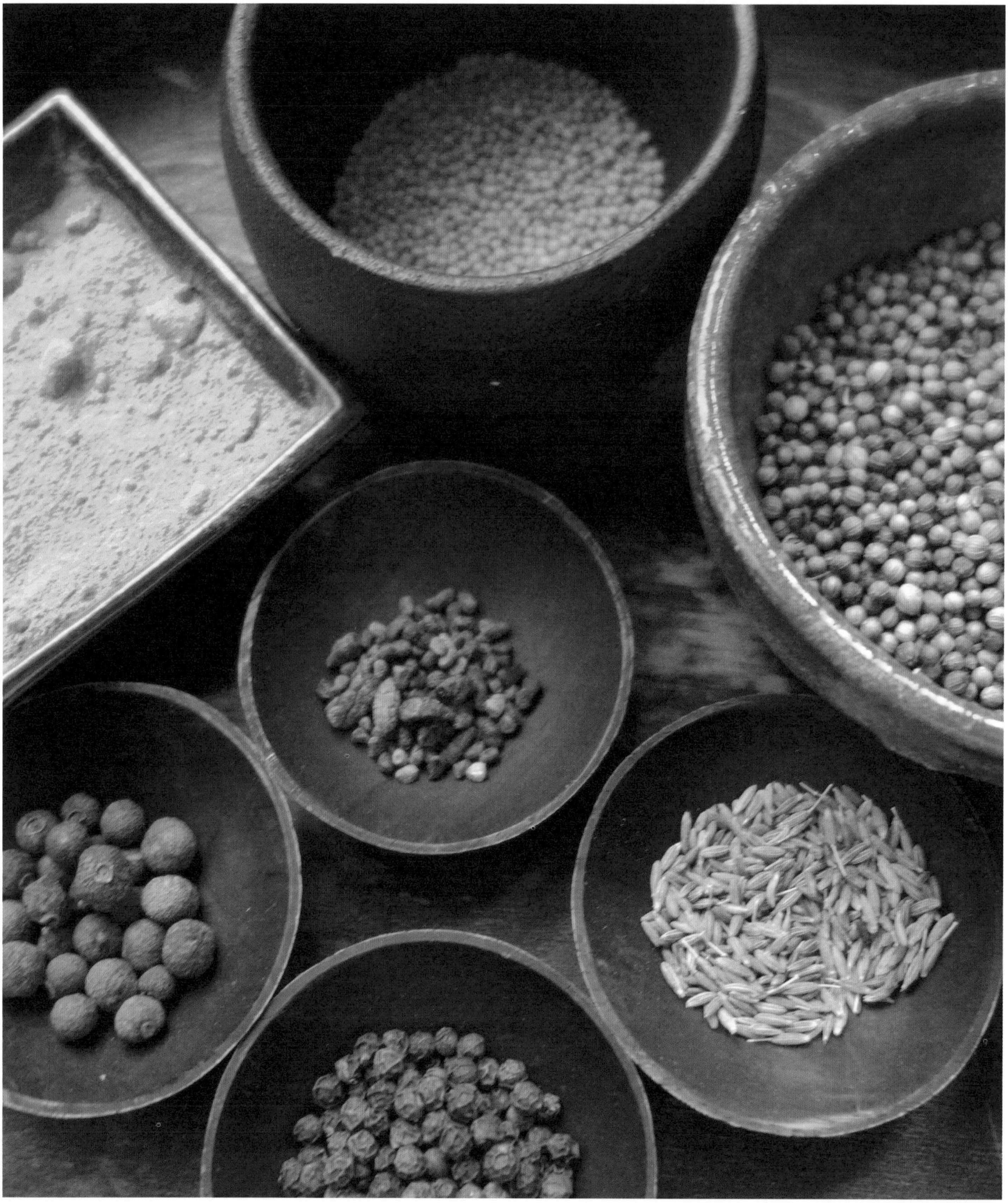

Curry Powder.

Kitchiner said that: *'This receipt was an attempt to imitate some of the best Indian curry powder, selected for me by a friend at the India house: the flavour approximates to the Indian powder so exactly, the most profound palaticians have pronounced it a perfect copy of the original curry stuff.'*

He recommended that flavours should be subtle, believing that *'their presence should be rather supposed than perceived'* in order to achieve a *'harmony of flavours'*. He claimed that no-one had tried to teach the *'art of combining spices'* before himself, and he emphasised the importance of giving measurements of the ingredients, which many writers of the time failed to do.

Ingredients

(I have used approximately a quarter of the quantities used in the original recipe)

25g coriander seeds

25g turmeric

I teaspoon of black peppercorns

1 teaspoon of mustard seeds

1 teaspoon of ginger, ground, or fresh ginger, grated finely

Half a teaspoon of allspice

Half a teaspoon of cardamom seeds

Half a teaspoon of cumin seeds

William Kitchiner. 1817. The Cook's Oracle and Housekeeper's Manual.

Put the following ingredients in a cool oven all night, and the next morning pound them in a marble mortar, and rub them through a fine sieve.

Coriander-seed, three ounces

Turmeric, three ounces

Black pepper, mustard, and ginger, one ounce of each

Allspice and cardamoms, half an ounce of each

Cumin-seed, a quarter of an ounce

Thoroughly pound and mix together, and keep them in a well-stopped bottle.

Method

1. Place all of the ingredients in a frying pan and heat gently until they start to pop.

2. Grind or blend them all together.

3. Put the resulting powder in a jar with a tightly fitting lid.

Lemon Comfits.

Jarrin. 1820. 'The Italian confectioner.'

Take some lemon peel, and clear it from the pith, leaving only a thin rind, which you must cut into small threads like the cinnamon (cut it into little pieces half an inch long, as thin as possible); blanch and prepare them as the angelica, and finish in the same manner (blanch them in hot water, throw them into cold water, drain them off, and put them into syrup; boil them till the syrup comes to the pearl, take them off on sieves to dry in the stove, minding to turn them from time to time, that they may not adhere to each other cut it into little pieces half an inch long, as thin as possible.)

Ingredients

The zest of 2 unwaxed lemons, cut into thin strips

100g sugar

200ml water

Method

1. Put the lemon zest into boiling water, drain then put into cold water. Drain again.

2. Dissolve the sugar in 200ml water then boil for 10 minutes. This makes a syrup.

3. Put the lemon zest into the syrup and boil for 10 minutes.

4. Pass this through a sieve then spread the zest over baking paper on a metal tray. Place the tray in a low oven at 100°c, gas ½, for about an hour. The lemon zest should be crisp and golden.

Lemons Pickled.

Charlotte Mason included a list of spices in her book, and also introduced ingredients that some cooks might not recognise, such as ginger: *'The best comes from Calcutta, but very good from many other places. It is dug up in Autumn, then washed, and spread on thin hurdles, supported on tressels. That which is sound, and of the deepest yellow, is best.'*

Charlotte Mason. 1773. 'The Lady's Assistant.'

They should be small, and thick rind; rub them with a piece of flannel, slit them in four parts, a little above half way down, but not through to the pulp; fill the slits hard with salt, set them upright in a pan, let them stand four days, or longer if the salt is not melted; turn them three times a day in their own liquor till they are tender: make a pickle of rape vinegar, the brine from the lemons, Jamaica pepper and ginger; boil and scum it; when cold put it to the lemons, with two ounces of mustard-seed, three cloves of garlic: this is sufficient for six lemons.

Ingredients

(I used one third of the quantities in the original recipe)

2 unwaxed lemons

50g salt

200ml cider vinegar or white wine vinegar

Half a chilli

12-15g fresh ginger, sliced

1 clove garlic

25g mustard seeds

Method

1. Cut the skin of the lemon lengthways in four slits, from top to bottom, stopping short of the top and the bottom. The lemons should remain whole.

2. Press the salt into the slits then place the lemons in a jar, and pour over any salt that remains.

3. Leave for 4 days, turning them round several times. A fluid should form.

4. Heat the vinegar in a saucepan with the chilli and ginger, and the salty juice from the lemons. Bring to the boil then leave to cool.

5. Add the garlic and mustard seeds to the liquid.

6. Pour this over the lemons.

Mushrooms pickled.

Elizabeth Raffald. 1769. 'The Experienced English Housekeeper.'

Gather the smallest mushrooms you can get, and put them into spring water, then rub them with a piece of new flannel dipped in salt, and throw them into cold spring water as you do them to keep their colour, then put them into a well tinned saucepan, and throw a handful of salt over them, cover them close, and set them over the fire four or five minutes, or till you see they are thoroughly hot, and the liquor is drawn out of them, then lay them between two clean cloths till they are cold, then put them into glass bottles, and fill them up with distilled vinegar, and put a blade or two or mace and a tea-spoonful of eating oil in every bottle, cork them close, and set them in a cool place.

Ingredients

100g button mushrooms

4 teaspoons of salt

70ml vinegar

A blade of mace

1 teaspoon of oil

Method

1. Sprinkle the salt over the mushrooms in a pan, cover and cook gently for 4-5 minutes until heated through. Some liquid should start to come out of the mushrooms.

2. Strain off the liquid and dry them between two sheets of kitchen paper.

3. Put them into a glass jar with the vinegar, mace and oil. Cover and store in the fridge.

Oranges Preserved.

Oranges preserved in syrup were considered to be good for digestion so would have been eaten as sweetmeats called suckets (from the French 'succade' or candied fruit).

Robert Smith. 1723. 'Court Cookery.'

Take six large Sevil Oranges, cut the Peel in what Size you think fit; as you cut them, sling them into Spring Water, and set them over a Charcoal Fire, and let them boil till they are tender, shifting the Water two or three times, to take out the Bitterness; let the Water boil as you shift them, or the cold Water will harden your Peel. When so done, have your Jelly made thus: Take a Quart and a half a Pint of Spring Water, two Pounds and a half of double-refin'd Sugar, boil and scum it well, and then boil your Oranges in it at a quarter of an Hour; then put them in a Jelly Pot. You must boil up the Syrup three or four times, adding Sugar to it: keep your Oranges cover'd with the Syrup, and tie them down when cold.

Ingredients

(I have halved the quantities used in the original recipe)

3 oranges

500g sugar + 150g

Method

1. Cut the skin from the oranges and then cut it into thin strips.

2. Put these in a pan and cover with water. Bring to the boil then drain.

3. Repeat this process twice more to remove any bitterness from the peel. Drain.

4. Meanwhile, dissolve 500g sugar in 750ml water then simmer for 10 minutes. Add the peel then simmer for 15 minutes. Cover and leave to cool.

5. The next day, strain the syrup into a clean pan and add 50g sugar. Simmer for 5 minutes then return the orange slices to the pan. Cover and leave to cool.

6. Repeat this process on three more days.

7. Pour the orange and syrup into jars and cover.

Note: if you want to make candied peel, lift the orange strips out of the syrup and spread them on baking paper on a baking tray. Put this into the oven at the lowest possible setting for two hours to dry out.

Pine-Apple Marmalade.

'Syrups are liquids of a certain consistence, which preserve the taste of the juice of the fruits and flowers of which they are made; the finer the sugar used, the better, for the preservation of the syrup depends on its quality, and the degree of boiling'. (Jarrin)

For most people, pineapples were a rare treat. Parson Woodforde described having a pineapple for dinner in 1766, which was *'the first I ever saw or tasted.'* (1985. 'A Country Parson: James Woodforde's Diary, 1759-1802.')

Jarrin. 1820. 'The Italian Confectioner.'

Marmalades are a half liquid preserve, made of the pulp of fruits, of a certain consistence; no marmalades can be well made without putting, at least, twelve ounces of sugar to a pound of fruit; they must also be boiled to a proper degree. Take off the outside of the pine, cut the fruit in pieces, pound it in a mortar, and pass it through a hair sieve; weigh the pulp, and take for every pound one pint of syrup; boil it to a blow, add the pulp, and boil it till it jellies, like apricot marmalade: 'till it hangs on the spaddle like a jelly'

Ingredients

200g sugar

200ml water

1 pineapple

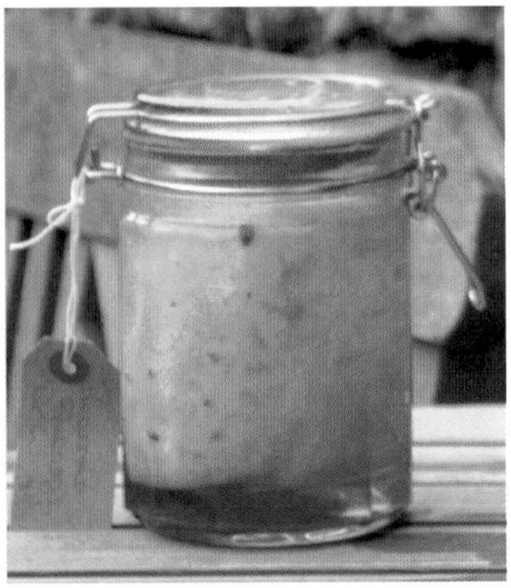

Method

1. Dissolve the sugar in the water and boil for 20 minutes until thick and syrupy.
2. Cut the outside layer from the pineapple, then cut the inner flesh into quarters lengthways and then cut out the core. Blend or mash the flesh fairly coarsely then add this to the syrup.
3. Simmer for 30 minutes until thickened then put into jars and cover.

Note: a spaddle is a wooden spoon or spatula.

Whole Pine Apple Preserved.

Pineapples were grown in special 'pineries', heated with furnaces. Unfortunately these sometimes burned down when the flues caught fire, which is why so few remain.

In 'Northanger Abbey', the general is proud of his pinery and succession houses (hot houses), whereas the unfortunate Mr. Allen only has one hot house *'which Mrs. Allen had the use of for her plants in winter, and there was a fire in it now and then.'* (1818. Jane Austen).

Pineapples were seen as a symbol of affluence because they were so hard to grow. They could be hired for dinner parties, to act as the centerpiece, at a cost of a guinea, if you returned it after the dinner. However, you had to pay two guineas if it was eaten by one of your guests!

Jarrin. 1820. 'The Italian Confectioner.'

Break off the top and stem of your pines, trim them well, and prick them all over with a fork, then put them into a pan of water and boil them till tender; take them out and put them into cold water; when cold drain them quite dry, and put them in a glass jar, or a pan; take syrup enough to cover them, boil it to a thread, and pour it on your pines; let them stand two or three days, then drain off your syrup, boil it a degree more, skim it well, and pour it over your pines; repeat this three days more, adding some new syrup as the pines imbibe the first quantity; the sixth day you must boil your sugar to the great pearl, then put in your pines and give them a boil up; take them off, skim them well, and put them in dry pans for use.

Ingredients

1 small pineapple

400g sugar dissolved in 400ml water

Method

1. Cut the skin, top and bottom off the pineapple and then cut it in half from top to bottom. Cut out the core then put it into a pan of water. Bring to the boil and cook for 30 minutes. Drain off the water and leave the pineapple to dry. Put it into a tall kilner jar.

2. Dissolve the sugar in the water then bring to the boil. Simmer until it reaches about 90°c. Pour this syrup over the pineapple and cover. There may be some remaining syrup. Keep this in another jar and use it for the second boiling. Gradually the pineapple will absorb the syrup.

3. Leave for 2-3 days then pour all of the syrup into a pan and heat to around 90°c. Pour this over the pineapple and leave for another 2-3 days.

4. Pour the syrup into a pan and heat to 90°c then add the pineapple and boil for about 5 minutes. Turn over the pineapple then boil for another 5 minutes. Put the pineapple into the jar with the syrup, or drain and dry it for immediate use.

Note: I reduced the number of times the syrup is re-boiled, to make it a less lengthy process. The result is just as good.

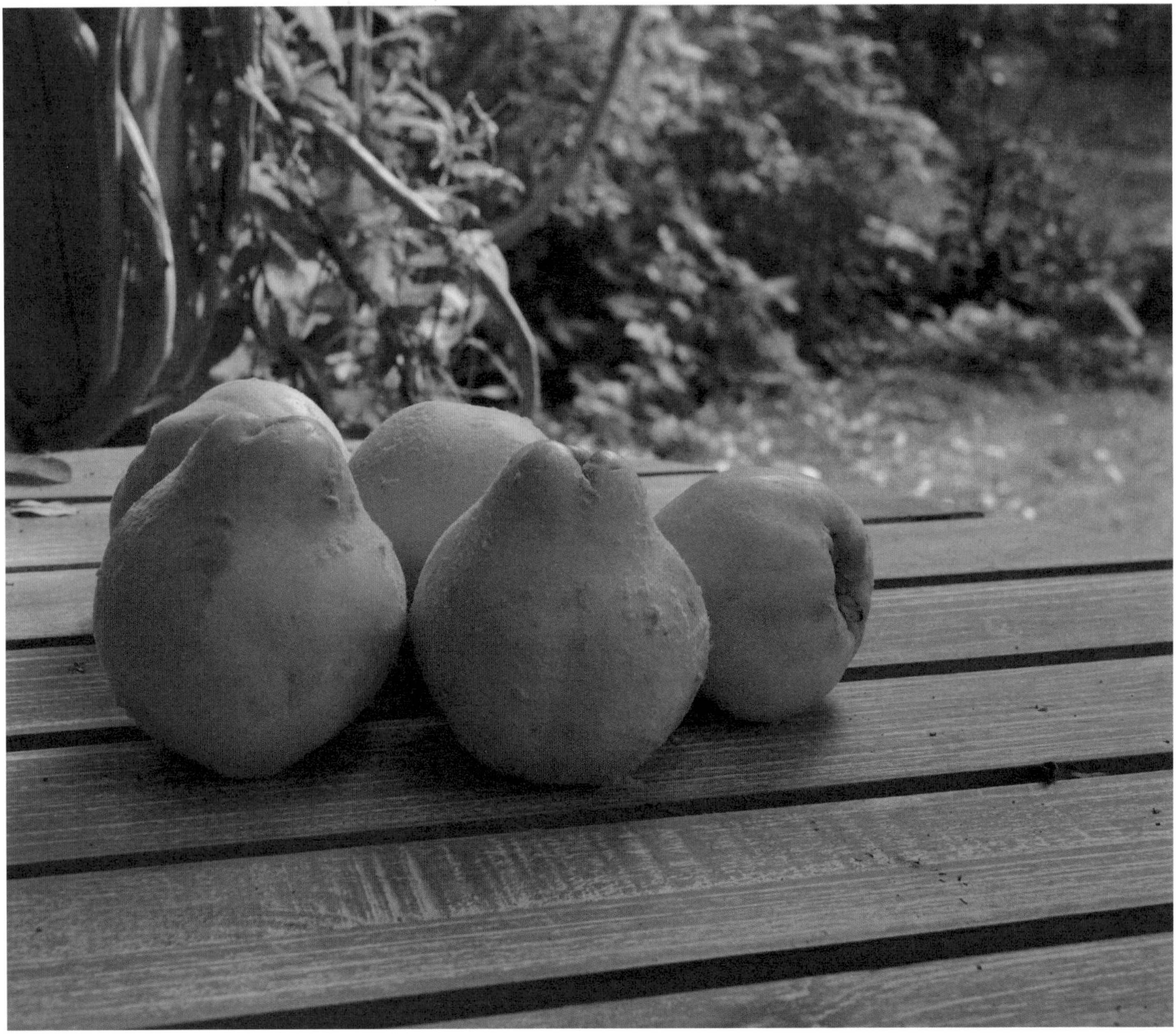

Quince Marmalade.

Marmalades at the time were made with quinces, producing a thick, dark paste, similar to membrillo. The name probably comes from 'marmelo', the Portuguese for quince.

Mary Kettilby, who published a collection of three hundred recipes in 1714, added lemon juice so that the marmalade would set to a jelly.

John Farley. 1792. 'The London Art of Cookery.'

Quinces for this purpose must be full ripe; pare them and cut them into quarters; then take out the core, and put them into a saucepan. Cover them with the parings, fill the sauce pan nearly full of spring water, cover it close, and let them stew over a slow fire till they are soft, and of a pink colour. Then pick out all the quinces from the parings, and beat them to a pulp in a marble mortar. Take their weight of fine loaf sugar, put as much water to it as will dissolve it, and boil and skim it well. Then put in the quinces, and boil them gently three quarters of an hour. Stir all the time, or it will stick to the pan and burn. When cold, put it into flat pots, and tie it down close.

Ingredients

3 ripe quinces, peeled and cored

About 400g sugar

Method

1. Put the quinces in a pan of water with the cores and peelings.

2. Cover the pan and cook them until they are soft and pink in colour. Lift the quinces out and discard the cores and peelings. Retain the water.

3. Weigh the quinces then measure an equal amount of sugar.

4. Place the sugar in a pan and add about 200ml of the water in the pan. Heat gently to dissolve the sugar. Bring to the boil then skim off any foam.

5. Blend the quinces then pass this through a sieve into the pan with the sugar water / syrup. Cook over a low heat for between an hour and an hour and a half, until it is very thick indeed and a dark orange colour. Stir regularly to stop it from sticking to the bottom of the pan. When you draw a wooden spoon across the bottom of the pan, it should leave a clean line in the mixture.

6. Put the mixture into a small, lightly oiled dish or tray and allow to cool.

Red Cabbage Pickled.

Francis Collingwood and John Woollams. 1792. 'The Universal Cook.'

Having sliced your cabbage crossways, put it on an earthen dish, and sprinkle a handful of salt over it. Cover it with another dish and let it stand twenty-four hours. Then put it in to a cullender to drain, and lay it in your jar. Take enough white wine vinegar to cover it, a little cloves, mace, and allspice; put them in whole, with a little cochineal finely bruised. Then boil it up, and pour it either hot or cold on your cabbage. Cover it close with a cloth till it is cold, if you pour on the pickle hot, and tie it up close, so that no air can get to it.

Ingredients

200g red cabbage, sliced finely

20g salt

200ml white wine vinegar

3 cloves

1 blade of mace or 1 teaspoon of ground mace

10 allspice berries or 1 teaspoon of ground allspice

Method

1. Mix the cabbage and salt. Cover and leave for 24 hours. Rinse and drain in a colander. Place in a jar with a lid.

2. Heat the vinegar with the cloves, mace and allspice. When it has boiled, pass the liquid through a sieve onto the red cabbage. Cover.

Strawberry Jam.

John Farley. 1792. 'The London Art of Cookery.'

Bruise very fine some scarlet strawberries gathered when very ripe, and put to them a little juice of strawberries; beat and sift their weight in sugar, strew it among them, and put them into the preserving pan: set 'em over a clear slow fire, skim and boil them twenty minutes, and then put them into glasses.

Method

1. Put 500g of the strawberries in a large saucepan and crush them.

2. Chop the rest of the strawberries and blend in a small food processor to produce a fine purée (this seems less wasteful than just using the juice)

3. Add this to the pan with the sugar. Heat gently, stirring until the sugar has dissolved, then turn up the heat and boil until it reaches setting point (drop a little jam onto a cold plate then push it with your finger; it should wrinkle). Stir regularly to make sure it doesn't burn on the bottom. Remove any scum as it rises to the surface.

4. Put into jam jars (this quantity fills two small jars).

Ingredients

600g ripe strawberries, trimmed

600g sugar

Bibliography

Cookery books:

Bradley, R. 1727. 'The Country Housewife and Lady's Director.' (Archive)

Briggs, R. 1788. 'The English Art of Cookery according to the Present Practice.' (Archive)

Collingwood, F., Woolams, J. 1792. 'The Universal Cook and Country Housekeeper.' (Google Books)

Farley, J. 1811. 'The London Art of Cookery and Domestic Housekeepers' Complete Assistant.' (Whittingham and Rowland,)

Glasse, H, 1747. 'The Art of Cookery.' (1997. Applewood books)

Harrison, S. 'The Housekeeper's Pocket Book and Compleat Family Cook', 1733 (1760)

Howard, H. 1717. 'England's Newest Way.' (2010. Ecco)

Jarrin, G. A. Italian Confectioner or Complete Economy of Desserts, 1820 (1827)

Kitchiner, W. 1817. (7th edition, 1830) 'The Cook's Oracle and Housekeeper's Manual.' (2006. Cosmo Classics)

Mason, C. 1773 (3rd edition, 1777) 'The Lady's Assistant.' (Google Books)

Martin, S. 1795. 'The New Experienced English Housekeeper.' (Google Books)

Nott, J. 1723. 'The Cook's and the Confectioner's Dictionary.' (Google Books)

Nutt, F. 1809. 'The Imperial and Royal Cook.' (2010. Kessinger Legacy)

Raffald, E. 1808. 'The Experienced English Housekeeper.' (1997. Equinox)

Smith, R. 1723. 'Court Cookery or The Compleat English Cook.' (2011, Lightening Source)

Verral, W. 1759. 'The Cook's Paradise: Complete System of Cookery.' (1948, Sylvan)

Books: fiction

Austen, J 1811. 'Sense and Sensibility.' (Oxford World's Classics)

Austen, J. 1813. 'Pride and Prejudice.' (Nelson)

Austen, J. 1815. 'Emma.' (Wordsworth Classics)

Austen, J. 1816. 'Mansfield Park.' (Wordsworth Classics)

Austen, J. 1818. 'Persuasion.' (Nelson)

Austen, J. 1818. 'Northanger Abbey.' (Penguin Classics)

Burney, F. 1778. 'Evelina.' (Oxford World's Classics)

Burney, F. 1782. 'Cecilia.' (OUP)

Defoe, D. 1722. 'Moll Flanders.' (Penguin)

Defoe, D. 1724. 'Roxana.' (OUP)

Edgeworth, M. 1800. 'Castle Rackrent.' (Oxford World's Classics)

Fielding, H. 1746. 'Tom Jones.' (Modern Library)

Radcliffe, A. 1794. 'The Mysteries of Udolpho.' (OUP)

Richardson, S. 1748. 'Clarissa.' (Signet Classics)

Smollett, T. 1748. 'Roderick Random.' (Penguin)

Smollett, T. 1771. 'The Expedition of Humphrey Clinker.' (Penguin)

Books: non fiction

Bayne-Powell, R. 1951. 'Travellers in 18th Century England.' (Butler and Tanner)

Bailey, N. 2015. 'Chelsea Physic Garden.' (Severn)

Barry, M. 1992. 'Great House Cookery.' (SAWD)

Berry, S. 2005. 'Georgian Brighton.' (Cambridge)

Boswell, J. 1950. 'London Journal 1762-1763.' (Penguin)

Boswell, J. 1791. 'The Life of Samuel Johnson.' (Penguin)

Bristol's Museums. 1998. 'Slave Trade Trail around central Bristol.' (Whitehall)

Buchanon, B. 2002. 'Bath History volume ix.' (Bath Archaeological Trust)

Dargan, P. 2012. 'Georgian Bath.' (Amberley)

David, E. 1996. 'Harvest of the Cold Months.' (Penguin)

Davidson, A. 2006. 'Oxford Companion to Food.' (Penguin)

Downes, K. 1979. 'The Georgian Cities of Britain.' (Phaidon)

Downing, S. 2011. 'The English Pleasure Garden 1660-1860.' (Shire)

Eden, F.M. 1797. 'The State of the Poor.' (Google Books)

Equiano, O. 1789. 'The Interesting Narrative.' (Penguin Classics)

Evelyn, J. 1699. 'A Discourse of Sallets.' (Gutenberg)

Gadd, D. 1971. 'Georgian Summer.' (Moonraker)

Hartley, D. 1954. 'Food in England.' (Macdonald)

Hickman, P. 1978. 'A Jane Austen Household Book: with Martha Lloyd's recipes.' (Readers Union)

Hope, A. 2005. 'Londoners' Larder.' (Mainstream)

Jakeman, J. (ed.) 2006. 'Ralph Ayres Cookery Book.' (Bodleian Library)

Jakeman, J. 2001. 'Kidders Receipts.' (Ashmolean Museum)

Johnson, S. (ed. Martin P.), 2009. 'Selected Writings.' (Harvard University)

Johnson, S. 1755. 'Dictionary of the English Language.' (Knapton)

Kelly, I. 2003. 'Cooking for Kings: the Life of Antonin Careme.' (Short Books)

Kenna, J. 2012. 'Quaking Pudding: A Georgian

Kitchen in Wales.' (Gomer)

Martin,P. (ed.) 2009. 'Selected Writings: Samuel Johnson.' (Harvard)

Melville, L. 1926. 'Bath under Beau Nash and After.' (Google Books)

Williams, S. 1993. 'The Art of Dining'. (National Trust)

Penrose, Rev. J. 1990. 'Letters from Bath 1766-1767.' (Sutton)

Powys, C. (Climenson, E. J. ed.), 1899. Passages from the Diaries of Mrs. Philip Lybbe Powys of Hardwick House: A.D. 1756-1808'. (Longman, Green)

Prochaska, A. & F. (eds.) 1987. 'Margaret Acworth's Georgian Cookery Book.' (Pavilion)

Rogers, B. 2004. 'Beef and Liberty.' (Vintage)

Rooney, A. 'The Story of Medicine.' (Arcturus)

Rotherham, I. 2014 'Spas and Spa Visiting.' (Shire)

Sands, M. 1987. 'The Eighteenth-century Pleasure Gardens of Marylebone.' (Bath Press)

Simond, L. 1815. 'An American in Regency England: the journal of a tour in 1810-11.' (Robert Maxwell)

Swift, A. and Elliott, K. 2004. 'Awash with Ale: 200 Years of Imbibing in Bath.' (Akeman Press)

Swift, J. 1745. 'Directions to Servants.' (2003, Hesperus Press)

Trusler, John. 1791. 'Rules of the Table.' (Google Books)

Turner, T. 1979. 'The Diary of a Georgian Shopkeeper 1754-1765.' (OUP)

Walpole, H. 1753. 'The Letters of Horace Walpole.' (Archive)

Watkins, J. (ed.) 1819. 'Memoirs of Charlotte, Queen of Great Britain.' (Colburn)

Whatman, S. 2000. 'The Housekeeping Book of Susanna Whatman 1776.' (National Trust)

White, J. 2012. 'London in the Eighteenth Century.' (Bodley Head)

Wilson, B. 2007. Decency and Disorder.' (Faber)

Woodforde, J. 1985. 'A Country Parson: James Woodforde's Diary, 1759-1802.' (Century Publishing.)

Articles

Accum, Frederick. 1820. 'A Treatise on the Adulterations of Food, and Culinary Poisons.' (Gutenberg)

Danby, Lady. 1725. 'Qualifications of servants and the business of each'. (Swinton Park. 1992)

Fox, W. 1792. 'An Address to the People of Great Britain, on the propriety of abstaining from West India sugar and rum.' (Archive)

Walpole, H. 'The Correspondence of Horace Walpole, with George Montagu, Esq.', 1779-1797 (Archive)

Wroth,W. 1896. 'The London Pleasure Gardens of the Eighteenth Century'. (Macmillan, Google Books)

Index